CUNARD

❖❖

Library

Out of respect for your fellow guests, please return all books as soon as possible. We would also request that books are not taken off the ship as they can easily be damaged by the sun, sea and sand.

Please ensure that books are returned the day before you disembark, failure to do so will incur a charge to your on board account, the same will happen to any damaged books.

THE HISTORY OF
EUROPE
IN BITE-SIZED CHUNKS

By the same author:

One Bloody Thing After Another:
The World's Gruesome History

We Shall Fight on the Beaches:
The Speeches That Inspired History

D-Day in Numbers:
The Facts Behind Operation Overlord

THE HISTORY OF EUROPE

IN BITE-SIZED CHUNKS

JACOB F. FIELD

Michael O'Mara Books Limited

This book is dedicated to the Bell Family,
the greatest in-laws anyone could ask for.

First published in Great Britain in 2019 by
Michael O'Mara Books Limited
9 Lion Yard
Tremadoc Road
London SW4 7NQ

A CIP catalogue record for this book is available from the British Library.

Papers used by Michael O'Mara Books Limited are natural, recyclable products
made from wood grown in sustainable forests. The manufacturing processes conform
to the environmental regulations of the country of origin.

ISBN: 978-1-78929-053-0 in hardback print format
ISBN: 978-1-78929-054-7 in ebook format

1 2 3 4 5 6 7 8 9 10

Typeset by K.DESIGN, Winscombe, Somerset
Maps by David Woodroffe

Printed and bound by CPI Group (UK) Ltd, Croydon, CR0 4YY

www.mombooks.com

Contents

INTRODUCTION

In simple geographical terms Europe is the western part of the Eurasian land mass, along with the islands in the oceans and seas that adjoin it. Europe's eastern border is fairly arbitrary – its border with Asia is usually defined by the Ural River, Black and Caspian Seas, and the Turkish Straits. This book begins five millennia ago, during the Bronze Age, when the first European civilizations began to emerge. It then extends all the way to the first decades of the twenty-first century. To allow the reader to gain an understanding of such a broad sweep of history, the book is divided into bite-sized 'chunks'. Each one explores an aspect of European history, be it political, social, religious, economic, or cultural. Some examine important events, themes, or periods in detail, while others provide mini-biographies of some of the 'Notable Europeans' who have shaped the continent. The 'chunks' can be read in isolation, but also form part of an overarching narrative.

An appreciation of the breadth and scale of European history is a vital factor in understanding the histories of the states and regions that make up the continent. They have never existed in isolation, and their interactions have done much to shape their development over time. These interactions have sometimes been violent but they have been outweighed by episodes of trans national collaboration and cultural exchange. Furthermore, while European powers no longer dominate the world through their empires and colonies, their legacy is felt everywhere; be it in laws, constitutions, languages, religions, or technologies. Europe's history still interacts with and impacts on modern politics; its legacy is inescapable.

The History of Europe in Bite-Sized Chunks will give the reader an understanding of the story of a continent where some of the most significant events in human history have occurred. There have been savage wars, selfless heroes, notorious villains, high-minded idealism, wanton violence, groundbreaking innovations, great works of art and numerous catastrophes. They are all contained within the history of Europe, and in the pages of this book.

CHAPTER 1

CLASSICAL ANTIQUITY

THE MINOANS

Crete was the centre of the Minoan civilization, a Bronze Age people named after Minos, the mythical King of Crete who kept a labyrinth in which he sacrificed victims to the Minotaur, a monstrous creature, half-man, half-bull. During the third millennium BC the Minoans began to make bronze tools and weapons as well as sophisticated glazed pottery and golden jewellery. They developed a hieroglyphic writing system (now known as 'Linear A') and traded across the Mediterranean, particularly with the Egyptians to the south. From 2000 BC the Minoans constructed a palace complex at Knossos, around which developed the first city in Europe. Later, they built other palace complexes on Crete, including Phaistos, Zakros and Malia.

Although a massive earthquake devastated Knossos in 1720 BC, a larger and more elaborate palace was rebuilt on the site over subsequent centuries. It was used for both administrative and ceremonial purposes, as well as housing workshops, residences and storage basements. When the complex was excavated by archaeologists in 1900 rich fresco wall-paintings were uncovered. Both secular and religious in content, they showed naturalistic images of animals, plants and people. One of the most famous depicts 'bull-leaping', an athletic religious ritual where the celebrants grasped the horns of a bull and then vaulted over it (a similar practice still takes place in south-west France). By the seventeenth century BC Knossos' population may have been as high as 100,000.

The Minoan civilization reached the peak of its influence in the sixteenth century BC, when it spread out to Cyprus and other islands in the Aegean as well as to the Greek mainland, where it influenced the Mycenaean peoples. In around 1500 BC Minoan civilization began to decline. One of the causes may have been a major earthquake off Crete's coast. This weakened the Minoans and allowed the Mycenaeans to conquer Crete and become the dominant force in the region. In 1400 BC a fire destroyed the great palace at Knossos; the city continued to be inhabited, but it diminished in both size and importance.

THE PHOENICIANS

Europe's first great commercial power was Phoenicia, which built a trading network that stretched across the Mediterranean from modern-day Lebanon to southern Spain. During the second and first millennia BC it established coastal trading colonies in the Levant, North Africa, Italy and Spain. Rather than being a formal empire, the Phoenicians were a loose alliance of city-states. Using their skill as navigators and shipbuilders, they traded in luxury items such as cedarwood, wine, ivory and glasswork. Some of their goods were transported as far north as Britain, where they were probably exchanged for tin mined there. The Phoenicians were most famed for their dyed textiles. The most sought-after and costly dye was 'Tyrian purple', which was made using the secretion of sea snails, and first manufactured in the city of Tyre (in modern-day Lebanon). It was so prohibitively expensive that only the elite could afford it, and the colour purple soon became associated with royal or imperial status.

For all of their economic might, the Phoenicians' greatest contribution to the development of European history was their alphabet, which was in use by the eleventh century BC. Unlike more complex systems that used hundreds of different pictograms or hieroglyphs to record information, the Phoenician alphabet was made up of just twenty-two letters. This meant that it was far easier to learn and use. As such, it became the basis for most Western alphabets, including the Roman, Greek and Cyrillic ones.

The Mycenaeans

From 2200 BC Indo-European peoples began migrating to mainland Greece. Thanks to their skill as warriors and weapon-makers they were able to establish tribal monarchies. They then solidified their control by building fortified citadels at strategic locations across the countryside. By around 1600 BC many of them had grown into cities such as Tiryns, Pylos and Midea. The most important of these early settlements was Mycenae, for which the civilization was named. The *acropolis* (from the Greek for 'highest city') there was constructed on a hill in the north-eastern Peloponnese that commanded the surrounding plains, and was protected by formidable walls made of stone blocks. The Mycenaeans also traded with nearby peoples such as the Minoans, who became a major influence, particularly on their artwork. During the mid-fifteenth century BC the Mycenaeans conquered Crete, supplanting the Minoans to become the dominant force in the Aegean with colonies in Cyprus, Rhodes, Italy and Anatolia. The Mycenaean writing system, now known as 'Linear B', spread across the region; it used around ninety different signs to represent syllables as well as hundreds of pictorial characters for objects.

Despite their strength and wealth, during the thirteenth and twelfth centuries BC the Mycenaean civilization steadily declined into instability and collapsed. Theories abound as to why this happened; one posits that it was due to foreign incursion, either by the Dorians from northern Greece or the Sea Peoples, maritime raiders who were the scourge of the eastern Mediterranean. It is also possible that internal disputes or natural disasters contributed to the Mycenaean decline. Regardless of its cause, by 1100 BC the Mycenaean civilization had disappeared as a major force. Their writing system likewise disappeared from use, as it was mostly used by palace scribes for administrative purposes (it would take until 1953 for linguists to decipher Linear B). For the next three centuries the Greek world was chaotic, unstable and illiterate. These 'dark ages' came to an end around 800 BC, with the rise of city-states like Athens and Sparta.

THE CELTS

The Celts were an Indo-European people who settled across Europe, from the Black Sea to the Atlantic coast, sharing similar languages and cultures. They first appeared in Central Europe in the thirteenth century BC, at which time they are known to have been making and using bronze, as well as cremating their dead and burying them in urns. Excavation of a site in Hallstatt, Austria produced a rich cache of artefacts and showed that by 700 BC they had mastery of iron, which was stronger than bronze. Thanks to their superior iron weapons and armour, as well as their skill as warriors and horsemen, the Celts gained control of much of the region, and established trading contact with the Greeks. The next phase of Celtic development was the 'La Tène culture' (named after a site in Switzerland), which began in the fifth century BC. Their distinctive and elaborate artistic style was characterized by abstract flowing, swirling lines. They also placed a high value on music and poetry. Although the Celts established some large fortified settlements, they were predominately an agricultural society. They were generally led by semi-hereditary kings and an elite warrior nobility. Their religious rituals and practice were carried out by professional priests called Druids. The fifth to first centuries BC were the greatest period of Celtic expansion, and saw them establish several independent kingdoms. During this period they migrated as far south as Spain and as far north as Britain and Ireland, even invading Greece and then venturing into Anatolia. The Celts raided south of the Alps into the Italian peninsula, and were a persistent threat to the nascent Roman Republic, sacking Rome in 390 BC.

GREECE'S GOLDEN AGE

By 800 BC Greek society had moved away from a tribal structure towards being organized into city-states (known as *poleis*). At first they were oligarchies dominated by a landowning class called the *aristoi* (literally 'the best'). Although each of the Greek city-states varied, they shared a number of characteristics, such as a notion of citizenship, an *agora* (open marketplace and assembly area), public trials, published legal codes, and *synoecism* (incorporating surrounding villages and countryside). The Ancient Greeks were polytheistic, with Zeus at the head of a pantheon of gods. However, each city-state had its own patron gods and festivals, which meant religious practice varied from place to place. The *poleis* fostered a tradition of militarism for self-defence and expansion. Their armies were largely made up of *hoplites* – male citizen volunteers who fought in a closely packed mass of spears and shields called the phalanx; victory in battle relied on discipline and trust in one's comrades. Many *poleis* had navies; by the eighth century BC they were using the trireme – a long slender vessel primarily powered by three banks of oars. Freemen who could not afford to purchase weapons or armour did their military service as oarsmen.

The most famed *polis* was Athens, which had been settled by 3000 BC. Under the Mycenaeans its famed acropolis was built in 1200 BC, and the city eventually grew to become an important hub of trade and brought the surrounding area (called Attica) under its control. Athens' growing wealth led to divisions between rich and poor, and caused internal tensions that brought it to the brink of civil war. To forestall this, in 594 BC the statesman Solon (*c.* 638–558 BC) wrote a new democratic constitution for Athens. It gave the poorest free men the right to vote for the *ecclesia* (popular assembly), which determined foreign policy, acted as a supreme court, and appointed senior officials and generals (who were generally aristocrats). Less important officials were decided by drawing lots. The *ecclesia* met three or four times a month and by the fifth century BC had grown to forty thousand members (six thousand were needed for a quorum). Over time, the majority of *poleis* copied the Athenian model, with adult male citizens actively determining and taking part in state affairs (Sparta was a notable exception). Although this democratic system proved fairly robust, in times of crisis sometimes an individual would take temporary power and rule without having to follow the laws or constitution – they were known as tyrants.

Not content to remain in their homeland many Greek city-states established overseas colonies. In total over four hundred were set up around the Mediterranean and Black Sea, spreading the Greek language and culture. Even when the political power of the Greek city-states declined, their cultural clout remained formidable.

Notable Europeans: Socrates (470/69–399 BC)

Greek culture during this period would make a lasting impact, particularly in the field of philosophy. One of the first great Greek philosophers was Socrates, who sought to find answers to fundamental questions, particularly how to live a 'good life'. The Athenian authorities found him guilty of corrupting the youth and not believing in gods; he was sentenced to death and, despite being urged to flee into exile by his supporters, submitted to his punishment, drinking a fatal dose of hemlock. His follower Plato (428/7–348/7 BC) argued humans had an innate sense of good and evil and in 387 BC founded the Academy, a school of philosophy in Athens. One of his students, Aristotle (384–322 BC), believed the world should be understood empirically, and so was a major influence on the development of scientific thought. Together, this trio are seen as the fathers of Western philosophy.

THE PERSIAN WARS

Greek colonial activity and interference in Asia Minor brought them into conflict with the Persian Empire, which ruled much of the Middle East. In response, the Persians invaded mainland Greece in 490 BC. They landed at Marathon and prepared to march on Athens, but were defeated by a Greek hoplite army, which forced the Persians to retreat.

The Persians returned ten years later, in 480 BC. This time they had raised a vast army (ancient historians say it numbered 2,500,000 but this is unrealistic – the true figure was about a tenth of that; still huge by contemporary standards), which was joined by a massive fleet. The Greek city-states put aside their differences to form an alliance, led by Athens and Sparta, to fight off the invaders. At the Battle of Thermopylae a Greek army of seven thousand led by King Leonidas I of Sparta (d. 480 BC) faced a Persian force ten times their size. Defending a narrow mountain pass, they held off the enemy for three days. This gave the Greeks time to regroup and prepare stronger defensive positions. Although Persia conquered Athens, Greece remained defiant. A month later a Greek fleet of 370 ships faced a Persian naval force more than double its size at the Battle of Salamis. The Greeks had cleverly tempted the Persians into a narrow bay where their numbers worked against them, and they were routed. The next year the Greek armies defeated the Persians on land, forcing them to return home once more.

The Athenian and Spartan leadership quarrelled about their next course of action. Sparta wanted to make peace with the Persians while Athens was eager to continue fighting them in Asia Minor. As a result Athens formed the Delian League, an alliance of other Greek city-states that shared this view, and carried on the war with Persia until 449 BC.

THE KINGDOM OF SPARTA

Sparta emerged as a city-state during the tenth century BC, and rose to become a great power by around 650 BC. Unlike other city-states it did not have a democratic assembly. Rather, it had two hereditary kings. Over time they became less powerful and acted as figureheads while the council of elders (*Gerousia*) and elected officials (*ephors*) became more influential. Sparta was highly militarized; all citizens were expected to bear arms. At age seven free men began a strict regime of military training (*agoge*) and they were recruited into the army at twenty. Spartan women also were given physical and martial training, and led the household while men were on campaign. Despite living in a fertile region, the Spartans did not generally farm themselves but forced the neighbouring population to labour for them. These people were known as *helots* – they were not legally slaves but as they were not allowed to leave their land the difference in practice was minimal. By the sixth century BC there were ten times as many helots as citizens in Sparta. To keep order, a secret police called the *Crypteia* was set up to monitor the helots and ensure there were no uprisings.

Following the defeat of Persia, there were two great power blocs in Greece: the Delian League, led by Athens, and the Peloponnesian League, led by Sparta. Tensions between the two alliances led to the First Peloponnesian War (460–445 BC). A second major conflict started in 431 BC. The Spartans advanced through the countryside around Athens but were unable to breach the city's walls. The war carried on until 404 BC when Sparta (which ironically had allied with Persia) defeated the Athenian fleet and forced it to surrender. This was a death blow to Athens' political and economic dominance, and made Sparta the greatest force in Greece. However, Sparta was not able to enforce stability in the region, and wars between city-states became more commonplace. This led to a power vacuum, which would be filled by the rise of Macedon.

THE RISE OF THE ROMAN REPUBLIC

According to legend, Rome, which was built on seven hills on the River Tiber, was founded in 753 BC by Romulus, who became the city's first king. Its monarchy was not hereditary – the king was selected by the Senate, an assembly of patricians (land-owning nobility). In 509 BC the king, Tarquinius

Superbus (d. 495 BC), was overthrown following a popular rebellion, which installed a republic. Roman political office was based on the *cursus honorum*. This was a sequence of elected offices that politicians were required to hold before they could become consul. Every year two consuls (who could veto each other) were elected to lead the republic. The system was not fully democratic by modern standards. Only free men could vote and bribery and voter intimidation were rampant.

In the two centuries after its founding, the Roman Republic expanded across the Italian peninsula. From the third to first centuries BC it extended control over the Mediterranean, defeating the Carthaginians in the Punic Wars as well as conquering Greece, Syria and parts of Asia Minor. Military strength played a major role in Rome's rise. At first its army was a part-time citizen militia, but as Rome grew it developed into a professional military. In 107 BC the general and politician Gaius Marius (157–86 BC) launched a series of military reforms. He standardized training and equipment, and insisted that veterans be granted land after serving. The Marian reforms created a skilled and motivated standing army. This proved a double-edged sword – some soldiers became more loyal to their generals than the republic, which would eventually lead to civil strife.

There were long-term tensions between the commoners (plebeians) and the patricians. This had led to the creation in 287 BC of a new elected office, the tribune, whose job was to intervene on behalf of the plebeians. During the 130s and 120s BC Tiberius Gracchus (*c.* 169–133 BC) and his brother Gaius Gracchus (154–121 BC) both held this post and sought to enact reforms to help plebeians. The centrepiece of their plans was wholesale land redistribution, but both brothers were assassinated by supporters of the patricians before they could achieve their goals. Civic politics descended into rivalry between the elitist and traditionalist *Optimates* and the *Populares*, who stood for the commoners.

Disorder characterized the 90s and 80s BC. The Social War (91–88 BC) saw Italian cities that had previously been Rome's allies rise up against it. They were defeated, but to prevent further warfare Rome granted citizenship to most Italian allies. One of Rome's leading generals in the war had

THE GERMANIC TRIBES

By around 1200 BC, during the later Bronze Age, the Germanic tribes, who were of Indo-European origin, had settled in southern Scandinavia and northern Germany. They then mastered iron-working, and expanded outward. One Germanic group, the Bastarnae, migrated as far east as the Danube delta by the third century BC. In 113 BC, Germanic tribes who had advanced south and west clashed with Rome. Two of them, the Cimbri and the Teutones, inflicted several defeats on Rome before they were subdued in 101 BC. Later, the Germans who had settled west of the Rhine came under Roman rule after Julius Caesar's conquest of Gaul, and many served in the Roman army. Rome never fully subdued the Germanic threat, and fought a series of wars against them that lasted until the sixth century AD.

been Sulla (*c.* 138–78 BC); from 88 to 80 BC he fought two civil wars to gain control of the republic, and conducted bloody purges of political enemics. This was a watershed; for the first time Roman soldiers had fought against each other in pitched battles – it would not be the last.

NOTABLE EUROPEANS: ALEXANDER THE GREAT (356–323 BC)

Macedonia was a small kingdom in north-eastern Greece that rose to become the dominant force in the region in the aftermath of the Peloponnesian Wars. From 350 to 338 BC its king, Philip II (382–336 BC), placed all of mainland Greece under his control. As Philip was preparing to invade the Persian Empire one of his bodyguards assassinated him.

Philip's successor was his twenty-year-old son Alexander, who had been tutored by the philosopher Aristotle. Alexander's conquests would go even further than his father's, stretching from Egypt to modern-day Pakistan. In 334 BC Alexander launched an invasion of the Persian Empire. He spent the next decade fighting in Asia and North Africa. Although he was often outnumbered two-to-one, he never lost a battle, thanks to his inspired leadership. In addition to his skill as a strategist and tactician, Alexander was also a master of logistics, ensuring that his men were always well supplied. By 330 BC Alexander had conquered the vast Persian Empire. Unsatisfied, he then moved on towards the Indian subcontinent, advancing to the Hydaspes River in 326 BC. At this point his men, who had spent years away from home, refused to go any further. Alexander was said to have wept because he could make no further conquests.

Alexander then settled in Persia; he began to adopt the local dress and customs and recruited Persians into his army and administration. This, together with his marriage to Roxana of Bactria (c. 340–310 BC), the daughter of a Central Asian nobleman, angered many of his Greek followers, creating tension between them and Alexander. Undeterred, he remained in Persia, and began planning an invasion of Arabia. In 323 BC, while he was in the city of Babylon, Alexander died. There were suspicions he was poisoned as part of a conspiracy against him, although it may have been a disease exacerbated by his years of campaigning and heavy drinking. After Alexander died his empire broke up – it was too large for one man to hold together. His leading generals divided the territory among themselves, starting their own imperial dynasties. The most enduring and powerful were the Seleucid Empire (312–64 BC), which extended from Anatolia to Central Asia, the Antigonid Empire (306–168 BC) in Greece, and the Ptolemaic Empire (305–30 BC) in Egypt.

CARTHAGE AND HANNIBAL

Carthage (in modern-day Tunisia) was founded by the Phoenicians, probably during the later eighth century BC. After Alexander the Great destroyed Tyre, another Phoenician trading city, in 332 BC, Carthage became a central hub of Mediterranean trade. Within a century Carthage was wealthy and powerful, with the largest harbour in the region. Thanks to its strong navy and troops recruited from local Numidian tribesmen, Carthage developed an empire covering parts of North Africa, southern Spain, the Balearic Islands, Corsica and Sardinia.

Rome and Carthage were drawn into conflict over Sicily, which had previously been largely controlled by Greek colonists. The Punic Wars (from the Latin *Punicus*, Rome's term for a Carthaginian) started in 264 BC. Rome built up its naval strength and by 241 BC had defeated Carthage and conquered Sicily. Three years later Rome annexed Corsica and Sardinia. Conflict restarted in 218 BC when the Carthaginian general Hannibal Barca (247–183/2/1 BC) launched a pre-emptive strike against Rome. He marched an army from Spain across the Alps and Italy from the north. He was joined by Italian tribes rebelling against Rome. At the Battle of Cannae, on 2 August 216 BC, he annihilated a Roman army, but was unable to capitalize on his success. Hannibal did not have enough men to capture Rome itself. Rather than try and defeat him in battle, the Romans launched persistent smaller attacks. Hannibal's local allies drifted away and he found it hard to gain supplies. In 203 BC he was recalled home when the Romans launched an invasion of Carthage. The next year Hannibal was defeated. Carthage was forced to make peace; paying the Romans a weighty indemnity and giving them control of Spain. Weakened by war debt and raids from Numidia, Carthage dwindled to a shadow of its former power. In 149 BC Rome, seeking to gain dominance over North Africa, sent an army to wipe out Carthage. After a three-year siege the city fell, and it was sacked and burned down.

Notable Europeans: Gaius Julius Caesar (100–44 BC)

As a young man Caesar fled Rome to avoid being caught up in Sulla's purges, and served in the Roman army in Asia Minor. After Sulla died in 78 BC Caesar returned and worked as an advocate, winning fame through his oratory. In 75 BC, while travelling to Greece, he was kidnapped by pirates; after the ransom was paid, he led an expedition to find them and duly located and executed his former captors.

Caesar then started his political career in earnest, winning increasingly powerful offices. Although he came from a patrician family, he was part of the *Populares* faction. In 60 BC Caesar formed an alliance called the Triumvirate with two powerful politicians: Marcus Licinius Crassus (*c.* 115–53 BC), the richest man in Rome, and Pompey (106–48 BC), known as *Magnus* ('The Great') for his military victories. Together they would dominate Roman politics. In 59 BC Caesar was elected consul; after his one-year term ended, he launched a military campaign in Gaul. Over the next eight years he subdued the Celtic tribes there and added the territory to Rome's. He also launched two invasions of Britain (in 55 and 54 BC) but did not conquer it, instead installing a client king.

Fearing Caesar was growing too powerful, conservatives in the Senate ordered him to return to Rome and give up his army. Caesar refused to do so and led his forces into Italy in 49 BC, sparking a civil war. The conflict ranged across the Mediterranean, from Spain to Greece. In 48 BC the war brought Caesar to Egypt, where he met Cleopatra (69–30 BC), who was fighting her brother over who should rule the country. Caesar and Cleopatra became lovers, and he ensured she was installed as Queen of Egypt. In 45 BC, Caesar defeated the *Optimates'* last army in Spain. The triumphant Caesar returned to Rome, where he was made Dictator for Life. He ruled without consulting the Senate, passing a raft of new laws. One of his most important reforms was a new calendar, which would remain in place across much of Europe until 1582 (in Russia it was not replaced until 1918). On 15 March 44 BC, as part of an attempted coup, a group of senators stabbed Caesar to death. Although Caesar had been killed, the conspirators would ultimately be unable to restore the old political order.

THE ESTABLISHMENT OF THE ROMAN EMPIRE

Caesar named his grand-nephew Octavian (63 BC – AD 14) as his heir. Octavian formed the Second Triumvirate with two of Caesar's chief lieutenants, Mark Antony (83–30 BC) and Marcus Aemilius Lepidus (*c.* 89/8–13/12 BC). They passed a law giving them dictatorial rule over Rome and its territories, and together they defeated the senatorial opposition by 40 BC. Octavian emerged as the leading figure of the three. In 36 BC Lepidus was stripped of most of his powers and exiled from Rome. Mark Antony, who had started an affair with Cleopatra, then fell out with Octavian. Fighting between them restarted in 32 BC, and Octavian emerged triumphant two years later. Rather than be captured and taken to Rome in chains, Mark Antony and Cleopatra both committed suicide, and Egypt was placed under Roman rule. Octavian had no serious rivals left and was able to do away with the old republican system. Although the Senate survived as an institution, it was unable to stop Octavian, who had a huge private fortune, popularity and the loyalty of his veterans. In 27 BC he was made Emperor of Rome. His new titles included *Imperator* (which came from the word *imperium* meaning 'power to command'), *Augustus* (meaning 'venerable' – a religious title, by which he became known) and *Princeps* ('first citizen' – a nod to republicanism). The rest of Augustus' reign was mostly peaceful, and lasted until his death in AD 14.

As Augustus did not have a son, his succession was at first unclear. To prevent disorder he designated his stepson Tiberius (42 BC – AD 37) as heir. Tiberius had been a capable general but after he became emperor he grew increasingly sombre and reclusive, often departing from Rome for his coastal villas and leaving administration to his lieutenants. He was succeeded by Caligula (AD 12–41), his grand-nephew and adopted grandson. At first the young emperor was moderate and popular but he quickly became a violent tyrant, and he was assassinated. His uncle Claudius (10 BC – AD 54) forestalled any attempts at restoring republicanism and ensured the imperial system remained in place. After Claudius died, his adopted son, Nero (AD 37–68), succeeded him. Nero grew cruel, even ordering the death of his mother. His extravagance and callousness led to revolt, forcing him to give up his throne and commit suicide.

Nero's death ended the 'Julio-Claudian' dynasty. It was followed by the political upheaval of the Year of the Four Emperors in AD 69. Coups, usually backed by military strength, became common features of the Roman Empire.

Despite occasional instability, the empire was held together for centuries by its strong and robust institutions such as its bureaucracy, transport infrastructure (its network of roads covered around 250,000 miles) and legal system. The backbone of the empire was the Imperial Army. Its main unit was the legion; made up of five thousand infantrymen who were Roman citizens who had volunteered for twenty-five years, and were highly disciplined and well supplied. At its peak the Imperial Army had around thirty legions. Non-citizens could join the army as *auxilia* (mostly light infantry, archers and cavalry), who numbered over 300,000 at their greatest.

The Spread of Christianity

Sometime between 7 and 2 BC Jesus of Nazareth was born in Judea, which became a Roman province in AD 6. Jesus began preaching and attracting followers; his ministry concerned Roman authorities, who saw him as a threat to their rule. In around AD 30 Jesus was crucified in Jerusalem on the orders of the Roman governor. This did not stop the growth of the religion his teachings inspired – Christianity. After Jesus' death his disciples spread his message, venturing out from Judea into the rest of the Middle East and the Mediterranean. At first, the vast majority of Christians were Jewish, but after the Council of Jerusalem (*c.* AD 50) it was decided that people from other communities could convert.

An important figure in the early Church was St Paul of Tarsus (*c.* AD 5–67), an Anatolian Jew who had persecuted Christians. After he experienced a dazzling vision of Jesus while travelling from Jerusalem to Damascus, he became wholly devoted to Christianity. As Paul was a Roman citizen he could travel across the empire, preaching, writing letters setting out some of the key tenets of Christianity, and establishing churches. One of Jesus' apostles, St Peter (d. *c.* AD 68), travelled to Rome, where he founded a church with Paul. Catholics acknowledge Peter as the first pope. He was executed on Nero's orders; one account of his martyrdom records he asked to be crucified upside down because he did not deem himself worthy to die in the same way as Jesus. Paul also died in Rome. He was arrested while preaching in Jerusalem; rather than stand trial, he demanded that, as a citizen, he be taken to Rome to appeal to the emperor. Like Peter, he was executed on Nero's orders, although he was probably beheaded rather than crucified. Despite the loss of two of its leading figures, Christianity's message of eternal salvation in the afterlife meant it steadily won followers across the Roman world (and beyond), particularly in cities and among the poor. Christians faced persecution by communities who thought their presence caused misfortune. In addition, Roman imperial authorities associated Christians with disorder, and accused them of being disobedient to the emperor.

Over time Christianity became more codified and organized. During the second half of the first century AD, the New Testament was written and collected together, recording the life of Jesus and the history of the early Church. To clarify and determine doctrine numerous councils were held where Church leaders and theologians debated matters of faith. Furthermore, by the second century AD an ecclesiastical hierarchy had emerged, with the bishops of large cities such as Antioch, Rome and Alexandria claiming authority over the surrounding regions.

The Roman Empire at Its Peak

The Year of the Four Emperors ended with the general Vespasian (AD 9–79) being declared emperor by his legions in AD 69. He ruled for a decade, restoring order and beginning a run of mostly capable emperors that lasted for over a century. This period saw the Roman Empire enter a period of relative peace and prosperity. Roman colonization delivered many benefits – roads, architecture, hygiene and trade, to name a few (it should be remembered that much of this relied on slaves, who made up at least one tenth of the population). An important tool used to tie together the Roman Empire was granting legal rights to some people in allied and conquered regions (only local elites tended to be given full citizenship). Roman citizens were protected under imperial laws, and guaranteed the right to trial.

The Roman Empire reached its largest size in AD 117 under Trajan (AD 53–117), a general born in Spain who became emperor with the support of the army. Trajan oversaw victory in the Dacian Wars (AD 101–2 and 105–6), which saw Rome extend its empire further into the Balkans. He then turned his attentions east, fighting the Parthian Empire (which covered much of modern-day Iran and Iraq), sacking its capital and annexing some territory. After this triumph, Trajan, whose health had been in decline, died in Asia Minor while travelling back to Rome.

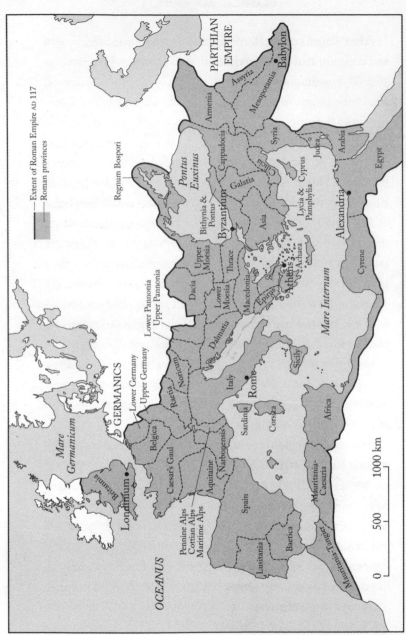

The Roman Empire at its greatest extent, AD 117

After Trajan's reign, Rome tended to avoid wars of conquest, and concentrated more on defending its frontiers. Hadrian (AD 76–138), Trajan's cousin, adopted son, and successor as emperor, abandoned some of the recent conquests. He initiated a policy of strengthening and extending Rome's border defences, ordering the construction of walls, forts and towers. Hadrian undertook an extensive personal tour of his empire, visiting Britannia, North Africa, Greece, Asia Minor and the Middle East, inspecting troops and investigating local issues. Symbolic of his policy of retrenchment was his eponymous wall, a seventy-three-mile-long stone fortification built from AD 122 to 128 that protected northern Britannia from the tribes to the north. Even more extensive was the *Limes Germanicus* ('Germanic frontier'), a series of fortifications that combined with the natural barriers of the Danube and Rhine rivers to prevent incursions from Germanic tribes into the empire.

Disorder returned under Commodus (AD 161–192), who scandalized Rome by fighting as a gladiator in the arena (sometimes appearing as the god Hercules), killing hundreds of exotic animals including ostriches, lions and a giraffe. His increasingly megalomaniacal tendencies, which saw him rename Rome *Colonia Commodiana* ('Colony of Commodus'), led to his death in AD 192. A group of his advisors turned against him and sent his favourite wrestler to strangle him while he was having a bath. The removal of Commodus did not bring order, but led to civil war and the Year of the Five Emperors (AD 193). As the Roman Empire moved into the third century AD, long-term political stability would become more and more elusive.

The Division of the Empire

From the early third century AD barracks emperors, who seized power with the support of their legions, became more common; from AD 235 to 284 there were fourteen of them. Their reigns tended to be short, usually no more than a couple of years, because if they lost the support of their soldiers they were vulnerable to being murdered by one of them or overthrown by a rival. In AD 284, Diocletian (AD 244–311), was proclaimed emperor by his soldiers. He reigned for over two decades. Ruthless and autocratic, he restored order by purging his enemies and putting down revolts. From AD 303 to 311 Diocletian instigated the Great Persecution, in which he subjected Christians to state violence and harshly limited their legal rights.

Diocletian's greatest legacy was splitting up the Roman Empire. In AD 286 he appointed a co-emperor to rule the western part of the empire. In AD 293 Diocletian further devolved power by dividing the empire into four (this arrangement was known as the Tetrarchy – 'rule of four'), with a senior and junior emperor (titled the Augustus and the Caesar, respectively) in both east and west. Administrative centres such as Milan in northern Italy, Nicomedia in Anatolia, Trier in Gaul, and Sirmium in the Danube region were established in peripheral areas, enabling closer monitoring of imperial frontiers. The eastern and western parts of the Roman Empire became increasingly separate, both politically and culturally (in the east, Greek tended to be spoken rather than Latin). Although the empire was occasionally reunited, this division consistently re-emerged.

NOTABLE EUROPEANS: CONSTANTINE THE GREAT (C. AD 272–337)

The son of the western Augustus, Constantine was proclaimed emperor in York by his father's legions. The Roman Empire then entered a period of civil war and rebellions, with rival emperors fighting for dominance. Constantine's main opponent in the west was Maxentius (c. AD 278–312). In AD 312, after marching an army into Italy to meet him, Constantine won a decisive victory at the Milvian Bridge, outside Rome. Before the battle Constantine was said to have received instructions in a dream to mark the Christian 'Chi Rho' (made by superimposing these two Greek letters on each other to signify Christ) symbol on their shields. Another account records that Constantine saw a cross of light in the sky just before the battle, accompanied by the words 'in this sign, you will conquer'.

Constantine was now master of the Western empire. The next year he and the Eastern emperor Licinius (AD 263–325) declared the Edict of Milan. This granted Christians (and all other religions) freedom of worship. Constantine and Licinius eventually fell out, and civil war erupted between them in AD 324. Constantine was victorious, and proclaimed himself ruler of both halves of the Roman Empire. The city of Byzantium, re-founded by him as Constantinople that year, became the capital of the Eastern empire. Following a rapid building campaign, six years later the city was consecrated as the 'New Rome'.

Constantine's support of Christianity was crucial, ensuring its survival and growth. He also had a major impact on its theological development; in AD 325 he convened the First Council of Nicaea, a great meeting of Church leaders held to establish a consensus in Christianity by settling issues such as the date of Easter. Constantine fell ill in AD 337; perhaps wishing to gain absolution for as many sins as possible, he was baptized on his deathbed (he had wanted to emulate Christ by being baptized in the River Jordan but his sickness prevented this). Despite his backing of the faith, Constantine did not proclaim Christianity to be the state religion of the Roman Empire – this occurred in AD 380, under Theodosius I (AD 347–395), the last emperor to rule both east and west (the Kingdom of Armenia was first to declare Christianity its state religion, in AD 301). Christianity's association with the Roman Empire gave it both prestige and protection, and also meant that Rome would become the most important centre of the Church.

THE FALL OF THE WESTERN ROMAN EMPIRE

During the fourth and fifth centuries AD, the Roman Empire steadily weakened, particularly in the west. Political instability was only part of the problem; there were deep-seated socio-economic fissures. As the Empire grew increasingly urbanized (Rome's population had reached one million by the second century AD – no European city matched this until the nineteenth century), agricultural productivity declined. The densely packed cities were also unhygienic, contributing to outbreaks of plague. Taxation revenue became insufficient to pay for imperial administration and military control, so the government debased the coinage, which led to inflation. This meant trust in the imperial currency diminished , leading to a decline in internal trade.

During the fifth century AD, Italy was repeatedly attacked. In AD 410 the western branch of the Goths, the Visigoths, sacked Rome. Attila the Hun ravaged northern Italy in AD 452, and three years later Rome was again sacked, this time by the Vandals. The Western Roman Empire finally ended in AD 476 when Odoacer (AD 433–93), a Germanic general who commanded a contingent of foreign soldiers who served the Empire, overthrew the last Western emperor, Romulus Augustulus (c. AD 460–507). Odoacer made himself King of Italy without much opposition from the people of Rome. In AD 489 the Ostrogoths, the eastern branch of the Goths, invaded Italy. Led by Theodoric the Great (AD 454–526), they overran the entire peninsula. Odoacer fled to the fortified city of Ravenna, which the Ostrogoths were unable to capture. In AD 493 Theodoric offered to rule Italy jointly with Odoacer, and was allowed into Ravenna. It was a ruse; a few days later Theodoric personally killed Odoacer, before murdering his wife and son. The Ostrogoths would go on to rule Italy for more than half a century.

THE HUNS

The Huns, a nomadic people from Central Asia, migrated to Europe in AD 375. By the end of the fourth century AD they had arrived in Eastern Europe and were raiding Persia and the Eastern Roman Empire. Despite their military strength, the Huns were politically disunited and often lacked a strong ruler. This changed in AD 420 when two brothers, Octar and Rugila, began to join the Huns together, rising to become co-kings. In AD 434 Rugila died and was succeeded by his nephew Attila (d. AD 453), who co-ruled with his elder brother Bleda until Bleda's death in AD 445. From AD 440 to 443 Attila campaigned against the Eastern Roman Empire. He forced it to pay him the equivalent of 2,000 kilograms of gold to withdraw, followed by an annual tribute of 700 kilograms more. Attila then switched his focus to the west, attacking Gaul in AD 451 and ravaging northern Italy in AD 452 (he was unable to reach Rome). He then retreated east of the Danube and began to prepare for an attack on Constantinople. Before he could carry it out, he died. One account suggests it was after a wedding feast where Attila drank so much he passed out and suffered a nosebleed that choked him to death. Without his leadership the Hunnic Empire quickly disintegrated into rival factions.

CHAPTER 2

THE MEDIEVAL ERA

THE FRANKS

The Franks were a Germanic people who invaded Gaul in the mid-fourth century AD. With the collapse of the Western Roman Empire leaving a power vacuum, during the fifth and sixth centuries Frankish rulers won control of most of Gaul, western Germany and the Low Countries. Initially, the Franks were divided into tribal kingdoms; the ruler of one of them, the Salians, was Clovis I (*c.* 466–511). By 509 he had united the Franks, becoming their first king and establishing the Merovingian dynasty. Clovis converted to Catholicism; setting an example that spread Christianity across Francia.

After the death of Clovis, his realms were divided between his sons, as was Frankish custom. This led to decades of infighting between different branches of the Merovingians and the fragmentation of the original realm into smaller kingdoms. By the end of the seventh century, the power of the Merovingian monarchs had declined. They became ceremonial figureheads overshadowed by their 'Mayors of the Palace', a senior official who actually held power. In 680 Pepin of Herstal (*c.* 635–714) became Mayor of the Palace of

Austrasia, a Frankish kingdom in north-eastern France. Under his leadership, it won a series of wars, reuniting the Frankish lands. Pepin's son Charles Martel (*c.* 688–741) continued his father's work, centralizing power and resisting Arab incursions into Francia. In 751 Martel's son Pepin the Short (*c.* 714–68) displaced the Merovingians, establishing himself as King of the Franks and beginning the Carolingian Dynasty.

Notable Europeans: Charlemagne (*c.* 742–814)

Charlemagne was Pepin's oldest son. When his father died in 768 he only inherited half of Francia; the other went to his brother Carloman (751–71). Relations between the siblings were troubled, but just as war between them appeared imminent, Carloman died. Charlemagne took control of his brother's lands, and then began a series of military campaigns, often personally leading his army into battle. His greatest rivals were the pagan Germanic Saxons to the east. In over three decades of intermittent fighting he conquered much of western Germany from them, as well as forcing them to convert to Christianity. The tireless Charlemagne also annexed northern Italy, north-eastern Spain, Bavaria, Frisia and parts of Austria and Bohemia. On Christmas Day 800, the pope crowned him the first Holy Roman Emperor. He took the title to show he was successor to the Roman emperor, adding 'holy' to show he had the Church's blessing.

Thanks to his near-constant wars and the vast size of his realm, Charlemagne was always on the move. He developed

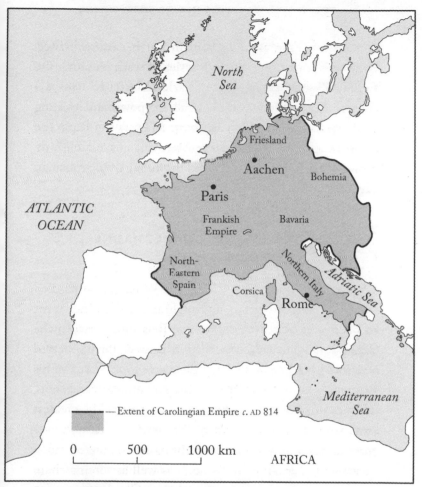

The Carolingian Empire under Charlemagne, *c.* AD 814

an effective administrative system, using a mixture of royal officials, local elites, family members and clergy to carry out his laws, keep the peace, collect taxes and recruit soldiers. Charlemagne was a great patron of the arts and learning, starting a period of cultural activity known as the Carolingian

Renaissance. His favourite residence was Aachen, which he made his imperial capital. He died there in 814 and was buried in the city's magnificent cathedral, built on his orders. Charlemagne's empire did not last long. During the 830s, it collapsed into civil war between his grandsons, and it was then split into three parts in 843: West Francia, which became the Kingdom of France in 987; Middle Francia, which stretched from the Low Countries to northern Italy and was partitioned in 855; and East Francia, which formed most of the Holy Roman Empire when it was formally established in 962.

THE BYZANTINE EMPIRE, 600–1100

In 600 the Byzantine Empire was the dominant force in the Mediterranean. At its centre was the emperor, known in Greek as the *basileus*. The title was not fully hereditary: although emperors often left their crown to their sons, in times of crisis they risked being overthrown. Defeated rivals for the imperial throne faced being forced to enter monasteries, blinding, castration or death.

Despite occasional resurgences, Byzantium declined during the medieval era. This began in the seventh century when it lost control of Egypt and Syria to the Arabs. Byzantine losses continued; between 827 and 902 they lost control of Sicily to the Arabs and in 1071 their last possessions in southern Italy were captured by the Normans.

During the eleventh century Byzantium faced a new enemy: the Seljuqs, an Islamic Turkic people. After establishing dominance over Iran, they invaded Anatolia in

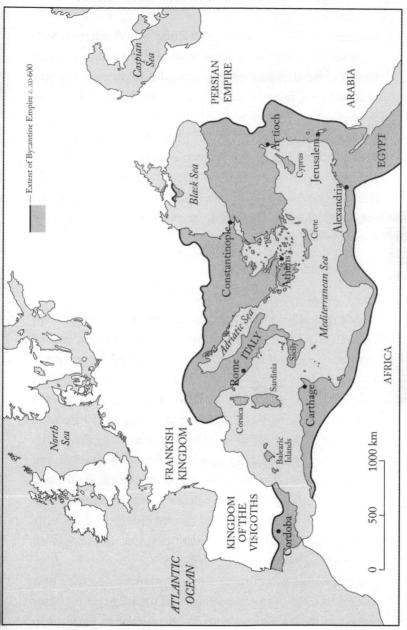

Extent of Byzantine Empire c. AD 600

The Byzantine Empire, c. AD 600

1067. On 26 August 1071, at the Battle of Manzikert, they destroyed the Byzantine army sent to defeat them, taking Emperor Romanos IV Diogenes (d. 1072) prisoner (he was returned to Constantinople but in his absence had been overthrown – Romanos was then blinded and confined to a monastery). Manzikert led to the Seljuqs taking Anatolia and the Holy Land. The Komnenian dynasty (1081–1185) restored stability and prevented further Seljuq incursions, but Byzantine rule now only extended over Greece, the south-eastern Balkans and a few Mediterranean islands.

The Slavs

The Slavic people probably originated in Eastern Europe, and during the sixth century they migrated to surrounding areas. Tribal at first, they later organized into several independent kingdoms and principalities. The Slavs divided into three linguistic and cultural groups. The West Slavs established themselves in Central Europe, where from the eighth to tenth centuries they established states in modern-day Slovakia, the Czech Republic and Poland. The South Slavs settled across the Balkans. The East Slavs spread across a wide area covering much of modern-day western Russia, Belarus and Ukraine.

Nobody influenced Slavic culture and religion more than the brothers Cyril (*c.* 827–69) and Methodius (*c.* 815–84). Respectively a professor of philosophy and an abbot, they were born in Byzantine-controlled Greece. In 862 they were charged with conducting missionary work among the Slavs. Their first task was to translate the Bible and other religious texts into the Slavic language. To do so they created a new writing system called Glagolitic script, which was designed especially for rendering Slavic languages. Based on the Greek alphabet, it developed into Cyrillic script, which is still used across Eastern Europe. In 863 the brothers set out to spread Christianity among the Slavs. Thanks in large part to their use of the vernacular language, the mission was highly successful and gained the approval of both the pope and the Byzantine emperor. The Slavs were largely Christianized by the tenth century but split between different branches of the Church. The West Slavs generally adhered to Catholicism while their southern and eastern cousins followed the Eastern Orthodox Church. Cyril and Methodius have been canonized in both Churches, and in 1980 the pope declared them to be among the patron saints of Europe.

THE ARAB INVASION OF EUROPE

During the early seventh century, the Islamic prophet Muhammad (*c.* 570–632) founded the Muslim religion and unified Arabic tribes under his leadership. After he died he was succeeded by a regime called the Rashidun Caliphate (from the title *caliph*, someone regarded as a successor to Muhammad). Over the next century, the Caliphate pushed into the Middle East, Central Asia and North Africa. Its success was helped by the fact that its two main rivals, the Byzantines and the Persians, were exhausted from three decades of fighting each other. More so than most other medieval regimes, the Caliphate was broadly tolerant of other religions in its lands; adherents were not forced to convert, although they had to pay a tax called the *jizya*.

Following a civil war between the Muslim leadership, a new family won control in 661, establishing the Umayyad Caliphate. They completed the conquest of North Africa, leading to the gradual conversion of the region from largely Christian to predominately Muslim. The Arabs then moved on to the Iberian Peninsula, which was ruled by Visigoths. In 711 an Umayyad army crossed the Strait of Gibraltar into southern Spain, defeating all opposition and taking Toledo, the Visigothic capital. In two decades they had conquered most of Iberia, establishing a territory called al-Andalus. They then raided north of the Pyrenees. In 732 a large expeditionary force was sent into Francia, meeting a Frankish army at the Battle of Tours, in north-central France. Charles Martel, the Frankish commander, achieved victory by securing the high ground and standing firm against the Umayyad assault before routing their army.

Tours is portrayed in some accounts as the moment that Christendom was delivered from an Islamic onslaught. The defeat was only part of the reason they ceased their advance into Western Europe. Firstly, there was a Berber revolt in modern-day Morocco that had to be defeated. Secondly, from 747 to 750 there was civil war within the Caliphate, which led to the Abbasid family overthrowing the Umayyads. The Abbasids established their capital at Baghdad, the greatest centre of learning in the world at the time and the hub of the Islamic Golden Age. Thanks to the work of scholars there, thousands of Europe's classical works were saved from oblivion by being translated into Arabic.

Despite disorder in the Middle East, Arab rule in Iberia persisted. In 756 an Umayyad prince who had escaped the civil war established an independent emirate that ruled most of the peninsula. During the tenth century its capital, Córdoba, became the largest city in Europe, reaching a population of nearly half a million. It attracted skilled artisans and architects, and new ideas and technologies were imported from the Arab world. Córdoba was also a great centre of scholarship, and it produced two of the greatest medieval philosophers: the Muslim Averroes (1126–98), who rekindled interest in the study of Aristotle by his commentaries on his texts, and Maimonides (1135/8–1204), a rabbi regarded as the most influential commentator on Jewish law.

THE REPUBLIC OF VENICE

Situated on a coastal lagoon in north-eastern Italy, Venice grew as a sanctuary for people fleeing Germanic and Hunnic invasion in the fifth and sixth centuries. In the early eighth century, the city elected a ruler, known as the 'doge' (from the Latin *dux*, meaning 'leader') and who held the office for life. Venice was originally under Byzantine authority, but by the ninth century was moving towards independence. At the northern end of the Adriatic Sea, the city had a prime location between Western Europe and the Byzantine Empire, and became a major trading hub.

Venice grew wealthier and more powerful after the late eleventh century. In 1082 it signed a treaty with Byzantium agreeing to assist in its conflict with the Normans. Venice received lucrative concessions, including the right to trade tax-free in the Byzantine Empire as well as its own quarter in Constantinople. By the thirteenth century, Venice had carved out an empire that grew to include Greek islands in the Aegean and Ionian Sea, coastal areas on the eastern Adriatic, and Cyprus. In the fifteenth century, Venice expanded into surrounding areas in the Italian mainland, but Venetian power declined in the sixteenth century, and they lost most of their overseas possessions.

The Venetians did not confine their activities to Europe. They looked further afield, to the Far East, where they were active in establishing trading links. Europe and Asia had been linked by the Silk Road, a network of sea and land routes, since the second century BC. Goods such as spices, pottery and silk went west while textiles, wine and precious metals were carried to the east. The most famous Venetian merchant was Marco Polo (1254–1324), who travelled through Asia from 1271 to 1295, spending most of his time in China. The account of his journey, entitled *Il Milione*, was immensely popular and its tales of the wealth and wonders of Asia inspired many European explorers and traders to travel there.

THE VIKINGS

In 793 Lindisfarne, a monastery off the coast of north-eastern England, was plundered by a group of seaborne warriors. These pagan raiders were the Vikings (also known as Norsemen). They originated from Scandinavia, where they lived in clan-based societies and were mostly independent farmers. From the ninth to eleventh centuries the Vikings raided across Europe, ranging as far east as the Caspian Sea, as far south as Spain, and as far west as Ireland. The

Vikings were skilled navigators and shipbuilders, capable of lightning raids thanks to their longships – narrow vessels equally at home in the open sea, shallow coastal waters, and rivers.

The Vikings also established trade routes that stretched all the way to the Middle East. From around 900 Vikings migrated to other lands. Some went west, colonizing Shetland, Orkney, the Faroe Islands, Iceland and Greenland, as well as establishing a short-lived settlement in Newfoundland in modern-day Canada, which they called Vinland. Others ventured east to the Baltic and Russia.

One of the areas which saw the heaviest Viking settlement was Britain and Ireland. From the later ninth century the Danes ruled much of northern England, until they were forced out by the local Anglo-Saxons led by the Kingdom of Wessex. England was once again placed under Viking rule in 1016, when it was conquered by Canute the Great (*c.* 995–1035), who made it part of his North Sea Empire that also included Denmark, Norway and parts of Sweden. However, Anglo-Saxon rule was re-established in 1042. Vikings ranged into France; in 845 and 885–6 they laid siege to Paris, and in the early tenth century their settlements in the north-west of the country formed the basis of the Duchy of Normandy. Over time the Vikings became more like the societies they raided; by the twelfth century most of the Scandinavian population had been Christianized. Monarchies replaced the old system of chiefdoms, and kingdoms were established in Denmark, Norway and Sweden.

THE NORMANS

During the early tenth century, Norsemen established settlements in north-western France at the mouth of the River Seine, giving them a base to attack inland. In 911, in exchange for an end to their raiding, the Carolingian king of West Francia conceded the land to them as a duchy. The territory became known as Normandy and the Norse leader Rollo (*c.* 860–932) became its first duke. The Normans intermixed with the local population, adopting their language and religion. They retained their ancestors' daring nature, spirit of adventure and the willingness to use violence, although they swapped maritime raiding for cavalry warfare. The Normans ranged across Europe in their quest of power and profit, and sometimes established themselves as kings of foreign lands.

In 1035 William the Bastard (1028–87), so-called because his parents were unmarried, inherited Normandy when his father died. His youth and illegitimacy led to a succession crisis as rival factions vied for control. After over a decade of disorder William solidified his rule. By this time Normandy had become highly involved in English politics, marrying into the ruling Anglo-Saxon dynasty. When Edward the Confessor (*c.* 1003–66) died childless, William, who was his first cousin once removed, claimed he had promised him the English throne. When his claim was challenged by an Anglo-Saxon noble, William invaded England and defeated him at the Battle of Hastings in 1066. William was crowned at Westminster Abbey and asserted his dominance by putting down local revolts and building castles to control the countryside. In 1086 he commissioned a nationwide land survey, known as the Domesday Book, which meticulously assessed the value of his kingdom. All subsequent English monarchs have been William's descendants.

The Normans were active in southern Italy from the late tenth century, initially serving as mercenaries for the Lombards and Byzantines there. During the early eleventh century they had established themselves as local lords, winning control of several small territories. From this foothold an ambitious Norman adventurer called Robert Guiscard (*c.* 1015–85) carved out a great kingdom. During the 1050s, he captured most of southern Italy from the Byzantines before he and his brother Roger (*c.* 1031–1101) conquered Sicily and Malta from the Arabs by 1091. Their successors ruled these lands until the late twelfth century.

THE CRUSADES

In 1094 the Byzantine emperor petitioned Pope Urban II (*c.* 1035–99) for help in his wars against the Seljuqs, whose conquests had disrupted pilgrimage routes to the Holy Land. Moved, Urban called a council at Clermont to appeal to people to join the struggle against the Turks. Hundreds of preachers went across Europe spreading the message. In return for going on crusade, the Church offered plenary indulgences (reductions in the afterlife punishment for their sins). However, for many the reason for taking the cross was an ambition for glory and wealth.

The first wave of people to set out was the 'People's Crusade'. It was a ragged force of around forty thousand, mostly without weapons or armour. Travelling on foot, they were ambushed by the Seljuqs in western Anatolia and mostly massacred or enslaved. The 'Princes' Crusade' was far more organized and included many powerful nobles. They left Europe by August 1096 and had gathered in Constantinople in April 1097. They then advanced to the Holy Land, where they captured Jerusalem in July 1099. They then sacked the city, massacring thousands.

The crusaders did not hand over their conquests to Byzantium, but established their own independent states (often known collectively as 'Outremer'). The most senior was the Kingdom of Jerusalem, but it never could extend its authority over the other crusader states, which included Edessa, Antioch, Tripoli and Cilicia. Outremer faced counter-attacks from Muslim forces, which steadily won back territory. This culminated in the loss of Jerusalem in 1187. Aside from a brief interlude from 1229 to 1244, the crusaders never won it back. Numerous crusades were launched to try and regain dominance of the Holy Land but none were as successful as the first. The last major crusade was the Ninth, which took place from 1271 to 1272. It was largely a failure. In 1291 Acre, the last major crusader-controlled city, was captured by the Muslims. The crusader presence in Holy Land ended in 1303 when Ruad, a small coastal garrison, fell.

To defend the conquests in the Holy Land, several military orders were created. The most powerful was the Knights Templar, founded in 1119. After receiving papal endorsement, they rapidly rose in power, peaking at around twenty thousand members. They were exempted from local laws, so did not have to pay taxes. This, combined with numerous donations and their trading and banking activities, meant they became wealthy and powerful. As the crusader presence in the Holy Land dwindled, Templar power also declined, leaving them vulnerable. In 1307 Philip IV of France (1268–1314) owed the Templars a fortune. Instead of paying it back, he arrested all of the Templars in France and confiscated their assets. In 1312 the order was disbanded.

THE NORTHERN CRUSADES

Catholic states had been fighting against the Baltic, Slavic and Finnic peoples to their east since the mid-twelfth century. In 1193 Pope Celestine III (1106–98) declared a crusade against pagans in northern Europe. This led to the Livonian Crusade, which saw German military orders, Sweden and Denmark conquer most of modern-day Estonia and Latvia, forcing the indigenous population to accept Christianity. The largest German military order were the Teutonic Knights. They led the fighting against the pagan Prussians and Lithuanians. As they were given the right to rule the territory they conquered, they established the State of the Teutonic Order in 1230, which covered much of the Baltic and existed until 1525. This period also saw Sweden subjugate pagan Finland, which it ruled until 1809. In the long term, the Northern Crusades were far more successful in establishing Christian rule than the campaigns in the Holy Land.

THE MONGOL INVASION OF EUROPE

After uniting under the rule of Genguis Khan (*c.* 1162–1227) in 1206, the Mongols established the largest land empire in history. After winning control of much of Asia, they prepared to invade Europe. After a decade of intelligence gathering, they launched their attack in 1236. They began by attacking the Rus', a Slavic people (although some sources claim they were descendants of Vikings), who ruled much of modern-day Russia, Ukraine, and Belarus, and sacked their capital city of Kiev in 1240. They then moved into Poland and Hungary; their advance west came to a halt in 1241, when their forces withdrew after the Mongol leader, Ögedei Khan (*c.* 1185–1241), died. This led to years of civil war over his succession. It also saved much of Europe from future Mongol incursions, as subsequent khans were far more interested in Asia. The Mongols retained control of Russia; this part of their empire was called the Golden Horde and split from the rest of the Mongol Empire in 1259. Its rulers settled the grazing land north of the Black Sea and did not occupy the rest of Russia. They forced the various Russian states to pay tribute to them and submit to their authority. Mongol domination continued until the 1480s, when the princes of a state called Muscovy began to lead a fightback. In 1547 they would declare themselves Tsars of Russia.

The Hanseatic League

By the medieval period, the Baltic Sea became a major trade route. It was primarily used to transport raw materials, such as salt, metals, grain, fish, timber and fur, from the Nordic region and Eastern Europe to the west, where they were traded for manufactured goods, particularly textiles. During the later twelfth century, northern German towns came together to conduct and regulate trade in the Baltic. From the mid-thirteenth century, they formed an organization called the Hanseatic League (the term originates from the German *Hanse*, which means 'association'). Around two hundred towns became members – they retained their independence but had to subscribe to a code called the 'Law of Lübeck' (after the city that was the League's central hub). Members provided mutual support by patrolling trade routes, building lighthouses and establishing foreign trading posts. Although the League developed a monopoly of the Baltic, it was not a formal federation; it had no permanent governing body or officials, and members met only once every three years. The League's power declined from the later fifteenth century as Russia, Poland and Sweden grew stronger and asserted their economic independence. In addition, English and Dutch traders expanded into the Baltic. By the end of the sixteenth century, the Hanseatic League was a shadow of its former self, and it held its last meeting in 1669.

THE HUNDRED YEARS' WAR

By the twelfth century English monarchs held lands in France that extended from Normandy to the Pyrenees. This caused tension and occasionally war with France, which claimed overlordship over the territory. During the thirteenth century, England lost most of its French possessions, and by 1337 was left with only Gascony. That year Edward III of England (1312–77) refused to pay homage to Philip VI of France (1293–1350). Philip responded by trying to confiscate Edward's territory in France, leading to war. Edward won a series of victories, such as Crécy (1346) and Poitiers (1356). France made peace in 1360 and accepted the English king's independent right to his French lands (which he had added to through conquest during the fighting).

War resumed in 1369. Under Charles V (1338–80) France recovered lost territory. Both France and England built up more centralized governments to collect taxes to finance the mounting costs of war. The heavy financial toll (as well as the destruction and death it caused) made it unpopular in both countries, leading to a truce in 1389. The final phase of the war began in 1415. France was in turmoil because the king, Charles VI (1368–1422), was suffering from periodic bouts of insanity (including believing he was made of glass). Henry V of England (1386/7–1422) took advantage of this disorder by allying with Burgundy (an independent duchy in modern-day eastern France) and invading. Following victory at Agincourt (1415), Henry brought England to the height of its power in France, occupying much of the country, including Paris. In 1420 Charles VI was forced to disinherit his children and accept

THE RISE OF THE OTTOMANS AND THE FALL OF CONSTANTINOPLE

The Ottomans were a Muslim Turkic people forced into Anatolia by the advance of the Mongols. The founder of their dynasty was Sultan Osman I (c 1258–1326), who founded a small kingdom that his descendants transformed into a trans-continental empire that persisted until 1923. The Ottomans first conquered Asia Minor before pushing into the Balkans and North Africa. Despite their successes they were unable to capture Constantinople from the Byzantines. Its triple ring of stone walls helped it hold out against Ottoman sieges in 1411 and 1422. In spring 1453, Sultan Mehmed II (1432–81) returned with a fleet and an army of over 75,000 that included several artillery pieces. The Byzantines only had a garrison of 8,000. Despite being outnumbered, the defenders stood firm until 29 May, when Mehmed launched a massed assault that breached the walls. The last Byzantine emperor, Constantine XI Palaiologos (1405–53), was killed launching a counter-attack. The Ottomans then sacked the city, which Mehmed renamed Istanbul and made his capital. The loss of the 'New Rome' was a huge blow to Christendom and allowed the Ottomans to move further into Europe.

that Henry V's sons would inherit the French throne. Two years later, both Henry V and Charles VI had died. Henry V's infant son Henry VI (1421–71) was hailed as king of England and France. Many in France rejected this, and declared Charles VI's son Charles VII (1403–61) their true king. He set about reclaiming his throne, and had an unexpected ally: Joan of Arc.

NOTABLE EUROPEANS: JOAN OF ARC (*c.* 1412–31)

Joan was a teenage girl from a peasant family who had received saintly visions that she should assist Charles VII. In 1428 England began besieging Orléans in north-central France. Its capture would pave the way to English dominance of all France. The siege was broken when Joan arrived with a relief force of five thousand in 1429 and drove the English off. This changed the course of the war and boosted Charles' claims to the throne. In 1430 Joan was captured by Burgundian forces, who turned her over to the English. In a farcical and corrupt trial she was found guilty of heresy and burned at the stake. Despite the loss of Joan, France steadily pushed the English back. By 1453 the war was over, and the English were left with only a small portion of land around Calais in northern France.

CHAPTER 3

REFORM AND ENLIGHTENMENT

THE PRINTING REVOLUTION

Printing was not invented in Europe. In China people had been printing on silk using woodblocks since the third century, were using paper by the seventh century, and moveable type by around 1040. All of these techniques had spread into Europe by 1300, but despite this books were still expensive because they had to be produced and copied by hand. This changed thanks to the German metalworker Johannes Gutenberg (*c.* 1398–1468). He married these earlier innovations with inventions of his own: a new metal alloy that made cheaper and more durable moveable type, an oil-based ink that stuck to the metal type and transferred to paper, and a press that would apply even pressure so the printed material would be more legible. After years of experimentation, Gutenberg's press, based in Mainz, was in operation by 1450. His masterwork was his edition of the Bible (based on a fourth-century Latin translation). Completed around 1455, it was an aesthetic and technological marvel – only twenty-one complete copies still exist. Gutenberg faced legal wrangles and financial troubles. Mounting debts led to a court ordering him to hand over his workshop and materials to his main investor. Gutenberg still continued to work as a printer and in 1465, in recognition of his work, the Archbishop of Mainz granted him an annual pension.

The impact of the Gutenberg press cannot be understated. It allowed for the mechanization of printing, which made books far more affordable and heralded the era of mass communication. The press could print 3,600 pages a day, and the design quickly spread across Europe. By 1500 it had produced over 20 million copies. This allowed for the rapid and accurate sharing of information, ideas and technologies.

NOTABLE EUROPEANS: FERDINAND II OF ARAGON (1452–1516) AND ISABELLA I OF CASTILE (1451–1504)

In 1469 the heirs to the Castilian and Aragonese thrones, Isabella and Ferdinand, married in Valladolid. This paved the way to the eventual unification of Spain into a single kingdom. Five years after the marriage, Isabella became Queen of Castile, although to solidify her position she had to wage a civil war to defeat a rival claimant. Ferdinand's ascension in Aragon (which also ruled Sicily) in 1475 was more straightforward. With both Ferdinand and Isabella ensconced on their thrones, they set about a programme of domestic reforms, which aimed at strengthening royal power (although Castile and Aragon mostly remained legally separate). They also created the Spanish Inquisition in 1478 to ensure the population followed Catholicism. From 1481 to 1492 Ferdinand and Isabella conquered the last Muslim enclave in Spain, the Emirate of Granada. Shortly afterwards their Jewish and Muslim subjects were given the choice between conversion to Catholicism or exile. Thousands were forced out of the country, and those who converted faced suspicion and persecution from the Inquisition. Abroad, the foundations for Spain's empire in the New World were laid as a result of Columbus' voyages to the Americas, which he claimed for Castile. Ferdinand extended the Aragonese realm by his conquest of the Kingdom of Naples in 1504, which gave him control of most of southern Italy. In recognition of their achievements the pope granted Ferdinand and Isabella the title of 'Catholic Monarchs' in 1494.

The Renaissance

Meaning 'rebirth', the Renaissance was a period of artistic and intellectual creativity from the later fourteenth to the seventeenth century. It saw a renewed interest in studying the ideas and techniques of classical thinkers and artists across a range of fields, from painting to sculpture to architecture to philosophy to history. Europe's nobility and royalty, realizing the prestige patronage could bring, supported the work of thinkers and artists. No patron was more important for the Renaissance than the Catholic Church, which commissioned countless works of art and buildings.

The Renaissance roared into life in Italy, which at the time was a collection of independent states and cities. Rivalry between and within them stimulated artistic advancement, as elites vied for prominence through patronage. As Italy was one of the most urbanized parts of Europe and a hub of commerce, there were many families wealthy enough to support artists and thinkers.

Artists began to portray people in a more realistic style, examining the human body so they could depict its form and emotions more accurately. Sculpture also became more lifelike, particularly the work of Donatello (*c.* 1386–1466) and Michelangelo (1475–1564). Renaissance architects and engineers studied the ruins of ancient buildings to emulate them. Domes and classical columns became popular, and there was an emphasis on symmetry and proportion. The most famed example of Renaissance architecture is St Peter's Basilica in Rome, the vast centre of Catholicism begun in 1506 that took 120 years to complete – it remains the largest church in the world.

No one personified the spirit of the Renaissance more than Leonardo da Vinci (1452–1519). Born near Florence, he became a master of an array of fields including painting, mathematics, anatomy and engineering. He spent most of his life in Italy, moving between Florence, Bologna, Venice, Milan and Rome. From 1495 to 1498 he produced one of his most famous masterpieces, *The Last Supper* (1495–8), a mural for a convent in Milan. As well as working as a court artist, he designed buildings and consulted on engineering and military projects. His notebooks included sketches for prototypes of a parachute, helicopter, and even a tank. He also studied anatomy – his published drawings of the human body were groundbreaking in their detail and accuracy. In around 1503, Leonardo began work on the *Mona Lisa*, thought to be the most valuable painting in the world. It was perhaps not completed until 1517. By then Leonardo had moved to France at the invitation of Francis I (1494–1547), who awarded him the title 'First painter, architect, and engineer to the King', and complete freedom to engage in whatever work interested him.

By 1500 the Renaissance had spread out from Italy across Europe; north of the Alps the movement was known as the Northern Renaissance. In the Low Countries – the location of major trading cities like Bruges and Antwerp – there were many merchants whose wealth enabled them to commission works of art. At first depictions of religious scenes were common, but over time scenes of daily life and landscapes became more popular. Artists in the region pioneered and mastered the use of oil-based paints, which allowed them to depict detailed, richly textured scenes with vivid colours. In Germany, artists often made printed woodcuts and engravings. The master of this technique was Albrecht Dürer (1471–1528) of Nuremberg, who became one of the most famous artists in Europe. The Northern Renaissance also had a major impact in France, England, Scotland and Poland.

RENAISSANCE HUMANISM

Inspired by classical thinkers, the humanists believed that people must be educated across a wide range of disciplines not just religion but also rhetoric, history, philosophy and poetry. They held that this would lead to an improvement in public and private morals, and encourage virtuous behaviour. Renaissance humanists were influential in religious matters, and critical of the abuses and corruption that had become rife within Catholicism. A core humanist belief was that it was desirable to study accurate versions of original texts, in order to help get rid of superstitious practices. This led to improved editions of the Bible and other religious works, including the first printed Polyglot Bible, which presented the Greek, Latin, Hebrew and Aramaic texts on the same page. It was sponsored by the Spanish cardinal Francisco Jiménez de Cisneros (1436–1517), and took from 1502 to 1517 to be completed.

The most influential humanist was Desiderius Erasmus (1466–1536) of Rotterdam. He was trained as a priest and was ordained but released from his vows so he could follow intellectual pursuits. He travelled across Europe, studying and lecturing at the universities of Paris, Cambridge and Leuven. Perhaps Erasmus' crowning achievement was his Greek translation of the New Testament, published in 1516. This was more accurate than previous versions, and formed the basis of later translations of the Bible into vernacular languages. Erasmus died in Basel; by this stage the Reformation had swung into action. Although he had helped to inspire this movement, Erasmus remained committed to the Catholic Church, seeking to change it from within.

Voyages of Discovery

At the same time as the Renaissance there was a drive to discover new lands and fill in the omissions in ancient geographical texts and maps. Although Western European states wanted to increase their political power and spread Christianity, the most crucial motivation was economic.

European powers were seeking new routes to both Asia (a source of luxury goods like silk and spices) and West Africa (for gold, ivory and slaves). Before the later fifteenth century, routes to both regions were overland – Europeans wanted direct maritime access. The first European state to finance intercontinental voyages was Portugal. It started with North Africa, before exploring the West African coast, trading guns and textiles for gold and slaves. From there the Portuguese sought a sea route to Asia. This was achieved by Vasco da Gama (c. 1460–1524), who from 1497 to 1499 sailed from Portugal to India via South Africa.

In August 1492, Christopher Columbus (c. 1450/1–1506), a Genoese captain in the service of Spain, embarked on one of the most influential journeys in history. Rather than sail east to Asia, he sailed west, arriving in the Caribbean that October, landing in the present-day Bahamas. Columbus believed he was in Asia (hence, he called the indigenous people 'Indians'). He returned twice more, with Spanish settlers who established colonies. This 'New World' was divided between Portugal and Spain under the Treaty of Tordesillas (1494). It created a line, to the west of which the lands were Spanish territory, and to the east Portuguese (which gave them Brazil, as yet unknown to Europeans). This treaty led to most of South America being divided between Spain and Portugal, but it was largely ignored in North America and the Caribbean, where France, the Dutch Republic and England also vied for control.

From 1519 to 1522, the first circumnavigation of the world was undertaken. This Spanish-financed voyage was led by the Portuguese explorer Ferdinand Magellan (c. 1480–1521).

He did not survive the trip – he was killed in a battle in the Philippines in 1521. This expedition established a sea route from the Americas to Asia, across the Pacific. Over the next four centuries European powers charted the oceans, establishing colonial regimes, usually to the detriment of indigenous populations, who were often exploited, enslaved or killed by Western weapons and diseases.

THE REFORMATION

No question was more central to Christians than how to get to Heaven, thus avoiding Hell. The Catholic Church held that the only route to salvation was through its priesthood and the sacraments they administered (particularly baptism, Holy Communion, penance and the last rites). Before ascending to Heaven, most souls would have to spend some time in Purgatory, where their sins were purged. Time there could run to centuries, but it was possible for this to be reduced though good works, donations and prayers. The living could purchase 'indulgences', which gave themselves or another individual reduced time in Purgatory. The most notorious seller of indulgences was the German friar Johann Tetzel (1465–1519). In 1516 to 1517 he travelled through Germany selling certificates of indulgence – his activities stirred the ire of a monk who taught theology at the University of Wittenberg: Martin Luther (1483–1546).

On 31 October 1517, Luther wrote *The Ninety-five Theses*. It attacked the sale of indulgences, arguing they were not a valid source of repentance. The document rapidly spread across Germany and the rest of Europe. This was the first division between Luther and the Catholic Church, which would turn into a permanent schism. Luther developed three main beliefs that put him at odds with the papacy: *sola fide* (that people were saved by faith alone), *sola scriptura* (that the Bible was the sole authority), and *sola gratia* (that only God provided salvation). Furthermore, in 1519 Luther stated that neither the pope nor Church councils were infallible. Luther argued that both laypeople and clergy should have a direct relationship with God (the 'priesthood of all believers'). To achieve this he called for the use of local languages (rather than Latin) in religious services and for Holy Scripture to be freely available in the vernacular.

Pope Leo X (1475–1521) ordered Luther to recant his beliefs – when he refused he was excommunicated in 1521. Luther was declared an outlaw but was protected by his local ruler, Frederick III, Elector of Saxony (1463–1525). Ensconced safely in Wartburg Castle, Luther produced a German translation of the Bible and many religious tracts. More and more people began to support his calls for reform, and questioned the teachings of the Catholic Church. Although he challenged ecclesiastical authority, Luther should not be mistaken for a political radical. When the German Peasants' War (1524–5), a popular revolt, broke out Luther condemned it, saying people should follow their secular overlords. He thus courted the favour of German rulers, many of whom came to follow his new faith. In 1529 Lutheran princes issued a letter of protestation against an edict that had declared Luther's work heretical. From then on followers of the reformed faith were known as Protestants. During the 1520s and 1530s, many German cities and states passed legislation that required all religious services to be conducted on Protestant lines.

Switzerland was an important centre of the Reformation. The key figure there was John Calvin (1509–64), a Frenchman who had fled his home after converting to Protestantism. He found refuge in Geneva, and in 1536 published *Institutes of the Christian Religion*, which set out the Protestant faith and its core doctrines. Calvin's most radical idea was predestination; he held that God had already decided who was to be saved and who was damned. 'The Elect' were destined for salvation and eternity in Heaven regardless of their actions. Calvin became the leading figure in Geneva, which was governed by his strict code of morality. Under his leadership Geneva became the 'Protestant Rome', and offered shelter to those fleeing prosecution. It also trained missionaries who spread their teachings across Europe – they were particularly successful in France, Scotland and the Netherlands.

The Catholic Church mobilized against Protestantism. From 1545 to 1563, a council met at Trento in northern Italy to debate doctrine and reform. Among other things, it was determined that Latin must be the official version of the Bible, that only the Church could interpret Scripture, and that people could be saved by faith *and* good works. Saints, adoration of the Virgin Mary, veneration of relics, indulgences and the sacraments were all retained. In 1565 the Tridentine Creed set out a new Catholic profession of faith, and created a liturgy that remained in place until the 1960s. Rome called for better training of priests, and opened new seminaries. New religious orders were founded. The most effective was the Society of Jesus, known as the Jesuits, established in 1540 by the Spanish soldier Ignatius of Loyola (*c.* 1491–1556). Jesuits were rigorously educated and highly effective as missionaries, political advisors and teachers. In contrast to the plain Protestant places of worship, Catholic churches adopted the ornate and rich Baroque style of art and architecture, which used lavish decoration and highly realistic detail, to encourage religious devotion.

The Reformation led to a permanent religious divide in Western Europe. Protestantism became the leading religion in England, Scotland, Scandinavia, the Netherlands, and much of Switzerland and the Holy Roman Empire.

THE HABSBURG EMPIRE

The Habsburgs became rulers of Austria in 1276 and, partly thanks to a series of dynastic marriages, expanded their realms to include Burgundy, Bohemia, the Low Countries and Hungary. A Habsburg was first elected Holy Roman Emperor in 1452 – the family retained the title until 1806. In 1496 a Habsburg prince, Philip the Fair (1478–1506), married Joanna of Castile (1479–1555), heiress to the Spanish throne. Their eldest son, Charles V (1500–58), was elected Holy Roman Emperor in 1519 and inherited the Habsburg lands as well as Spain and its territories in Italy, Asia and the Americas. Charles faced near-constant warfare. He fought France for control of Italy and struggled to hold back Ottoman advances into Central Europe. A devout Catholic, he also withstood the Reformation in the Holy Roman Empire, as well as struggling to control local rulers who wanted greater independence.

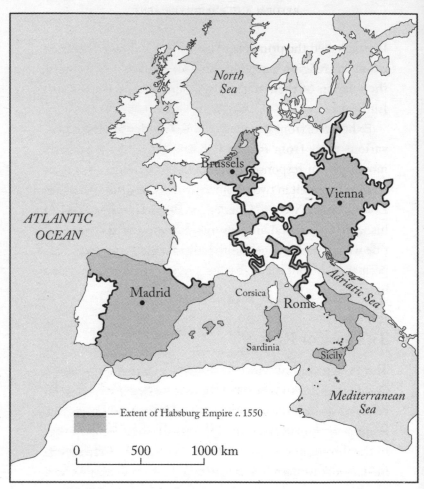

The Habsburg Empire under Charles V, *c.* 1550

After years of tension, the empire descended into war from 1547 to 1548. Although Charles at first defeated a Protestant alliance, this victory was temporary. In 1552 another alliance of German Protestant princes, with French support, overcame him. Three years later he agreed to the Peace of Augsburg.

It established the principle of *cuius regio, eius religio* ('whose realm, his religion'), meaning that local rulers could choose the religion of their states (it could either be Catholic or Lutheran).

Exhausted from decades of toil, Charles abdicated his various titles from 1554 to 1556 and retired to a Spanish monastery. In response to the stresses of ruling so vast an empire, he split it in two. Spain, its overseas territories and the Low Countries went to Charles' son Philip II (1527–98), while his lands in Central and Eastern Europe and the imperial title went to his younger brother, Ferdinand I (1503–64). This permanently split the Habsburgs into Spanish and Austrian branches.

THE RISE OF RUSSIA

The Principality of Moscow grew in size and prominence during the later thirteenth and fourteenth centuries, and its rulers fought off the Mongol Golden Horde to become the leading force in Russia. In 1462 Ivan III (1440–1505) came to the throne; known as 'the Great', he annexed territory in modern-day western Russia as well as parts of Ukraine, Poland and Lithuania, and laid the foundations of a centralized state. His grandson Ivan IV (1530–84), generally known in the West as 'the Terrible', continued this work. After ascending to the throne at age three, he was crowned 'Tsar of All the Russias' ('tsar' derives from the Latin 'Caesar') in 1547, the first of his dynasty to use this title. He ruled through a combination of intelligence and violence. During his reign Russia grew even further, as did the power of the tsar.

The Romanov dynasty, which ruled Russia from 1613 to 1917, turned the country into a major power. Their greatest figure was Peter the Great (1672–1725), who from 1682 to 1696 co-ruled with his half-brother Ivan V (1666–96). After Peter assumed sole rule, he spent eighteen months touring Europe. He returned determined to modernize Russia, and brought in foreign experts to help him do so. In 1703 he founded a new city overlooking the Baltic: St Petersburg, which became his capital in 1710. He limited the power of the Russian Church and nobility. Under his rule social status was based on service to the throne rather than birth. Those who resisted his reforms were brutally put down – most visibly, courtiers who refused to shave off their long beards had them hacked off by Peter. Russia's armed forces were brought up to date, and went on to defeat neighbouring powers like Sweden and the Ottoman Empire. Four years before his death, Peter gave himself and his successors a new title, 'Emperor of All Russia'.

EUROPEAN TRADING COMPANIES

During the sixteenth and seventeenth centuries, many European states encouraged overseas economic activity by establishing trading companies. These aimed to secure new markets for their country's manufactures, but their prime aim was to secure control of access to foreign goods, such as tea, coffee and chocolate, as well as tobacco. They were consumed at coffee houses, which sprang up in cities across Europe and became important sites for the exchange of ideas and information.

Some of the trading companies became powerful forces in their own right, even acting as local rulers of overseas territories. They were licensed by their respective national governments (which often granted them monopolies) but usually operated with a high degree of independence, as they were largely funded by the investment of citizens who had purchased shares. One of the earliest of these 'joint-stock companies' was the English Company of Merchant Adventurers to New Lands (later known as the Muscovy Company), incorporated in 1553 to trade with Russia and Persia.

The two most powerful trading companies were the English and Dutch East India Companies, founded in 1600 and 1602. They vied for dominance of the lucrative East Asian market, the source of goods such as silks, dyes, spices, tea, opium and china. Their rivalry occasionally erupted into open warfare. Their activities laid the foundation for later English and Dutch colonial rule in the Indian subcontinent and Indonesia, respectively. The Austrians, Danes, French, Portuguese and Swedish established their own companies to trade in the East Indies, but all were relatively small compared with their Dutch and English counterparts. European states did not confine themselves to Asia in their quest for profit and power. There were also trading companies specifically for North America, the Caribbean and Africa.

The Thirty Years' War (1618–48)

In the decades after 1555, there was mostly peace within the Holy Roman Empire, although there remained religious tensions. Conflict broke out again in Bohemia, ruled by the Habsburgs, who had largely allowed their Hussite and Protestant subjects there freedom of worship. In 1618 the Habsburgs began to move to limit Bohemian religious and political freedoms. As a result Bohemian Protestants threw three representatives of the Habsburgs out of a window in Prague Castle. Bohemia revolted and offered its throne to a German Protestant prince, Frederick V, Elector Palatine (1596–1632). Warfare spread across the empire. The first major battle of the war was at the White Mountain in 1620 – when an imperial army defeated the rebels and took Prague, forcing Frederick to flee into exile in Mainz. As a result Catholic powers dominated the war during the 1620s.

At first, the conflict was mostly between Protestant and Catholic states of the Holy Roman Empire. Foreign powers quickly intervened. The Spanish supported their Austrian Habsburg cousins from the beginning, while Denmark, England, Scotland and the Dutch Republic all offered the Protestant side support during the 1620s. The most important foreign intervention came from Sweden (which also ruled Finland). During the early seventeenth century, through conflict with Poland-Lithuania and Russia, the Swedes had carved out an empire in the Baltic. Sweden benefitted from being a comparatively highly centralized state, with a strong tax structure, and the ability to conscript their population. In 1630 the Swedish king, Gustavus Adolphus (1594–1632), invaded Germany. He was hailed as the 'Lion of the North' who would deliver the Protestant cause from defeat. His army (which also included mercenaries) was highly disciplined and featured infantry integrated with cavalry and artillery. Gustavus advanced from the Baltic to Bavaria, where he triumphed at the Battle of Breitenfeld in 1631. The next year he was killed leading his army to victory at Lützen, stripping the Protestants of their most dynamic leader. In the aftermath of Gustavus' death, France formally entered the war in 1635 on the Protestant side, as well as providing financial assistance to Sweden so they could keep their army in the field. They did so because they feared a Habsburg victory would leave them encircled by hostile powers. France also supported anti-Spanish rebels in Catalonia and Portugal. Although Catalonia remained under Spanish control, Portugal (which had been unified with Spain since 1580) regained independence in 1640.

Peace negotiations began in earnest in 1646, taking place in the Westphalia region of north-western Germany, which was declared neutral territory. After two years of negotiations, involving representatives from over a hundred states, the Peace of Westphalia was concluded (although Spain and France carried on fighting until 1659). The three separate treaties that made up the peace deal saw Spain formally recognize Dutch independence while Sweden was given a cash settlement and had its Baltic territory confirmed. Most importantly, Westphalia sought to stabilize the Holy Roman Empire. Local rulers had internal sovereignty over their territories recognized. The Peace granted religious freedom for Christians in the empire, and stated that Protestants and Catholics were equal before the law.

THE ATLANTIC SLAVE TRADE

Since the eighth century Muslim merchants had sold African slaves across the Mediterranean and Asia. After the mid-fifteenth century, Europeans became involved in the African slave trade, increasing its size and shifting its focus to the Atlantic. The first European slave traders were Portuguese. They were later joined by other Europeans including the Spanish, English, French and Dutch. Slaves were primarily used to labour on plantations in the Americas – the primary crop they were forced to cultivate was sugar, although cotton, indigo, tobacco and coffee were also important. The conditions they suffered in the crossing of the Atlantic were brutal and inhumane – around one third of the 12 million Africans Europeans enslaved died before they reached the Americas. At the trade's peak, in the 1780s, nearly ninety thousand slaves were sent across the Atlantic every year. Slave revolts and resistance were common and led to violent and cruel retribution. During the eighteenth century, the abolitionist movement grew in influence, as many questioned the morality and legality of slavery. In 1792 Denmark became the first European state to ban the slave trade, although the law did not come into effect until 1803; other countries followed, including Britain in 1807, Spain in 1811 and the Netherlands in 1814. However, it was not until the mid-nineteenth century that European powers began to abolish slavery completely in their overseas empires, starting with Britain in 1834.

Notable Europeans: Louis XIV of France (1638–1715)

After Louis XIII (1601–43) died he was succeeded by his four-year-old son, Louis XIV. As he was so young, his father's chief minister, the Italian-born cardinal Jules Mazarin (1602–61), ruled for him. After Mazarin died, Louis XIV assumed sole rule, establishing a system of absolute monarchy. The symbol of his authority was Versailles Palace, to which Louis XIV moved the royal court in 1682. Once a hunting lodge, it was enlarged by Louis into a vast complex of buildings and gardens. Everything focused on the central courtyard and the king's suite, which only the most favoured were allowed to enter. All power emanated from Versailles; senior government offices were based there and members of the royal family and nobles were expected to spend time there. Louis XIV's nickname, 'The Sun King', reflected his power, brilliance and centrality to the nation.

The Scientific Revolution

Modern science began to emerge during the early modern period, laying the foundations for a transformation in the way the natural world and the cosmos was understood. This process is known as the Scientific Revolution, which occurred during the seventeenth and eighteenth centuries. A crucial feature was the scientific method, in which people began to examine the world through systematic experimentation and observation. This spirit of empiricism was encouraged by the English philosopher and statesman Francis Bacon

(1561–1626), who argued that knowledge could only be gained through observation. Later, the French philosopher René Descartes (1596–1650) asserted that reason was vital to understanding the world. Scientific investigation was helped by technological innovations such as the compound microscope, as well as increasingly powerful telescopes, which enabled far closer observation of the heavens. Medical knowledge expanded as human corpses began to be more widely used for dissection.

The Scientific Revolution saw a radical shift in how humans understood their place in the cosmos. Traditional astronomy was based on a geocentric model, with Earth at the centre, orbited by the Sun and planets. In around 1514, Nicolaus Copernicus (1473–1543) proposed that the Earth actually revolved around the Sun. Although ancient astronomers had suggested this as early as the third century BC, Copernicus formulated a mathematical model to support his claim. His work proved highly influential, but it was deeply controversial for the Church. In Italy Galileo Galilei (1564–1642) used the telescopes he invented to confirm through observation the Copernican view of the cosmos. This led to him being put on trial by the Roman Inquisition in 1615, and he was forced to spend the rest of his life under house arrest.

THE ENLIGHTENMENT

A pan-European movement that started in the later seventeenth century and continued into the eighteenth, the Enlightenment challenged superstition and tradition. It

THE OTTOMANS IN EUROPE

In the century after the conquest of Constantinople in 1453, the Ottoman Empire reached the peak of its power. By the mid-sixteenth century it extended from the Middle East across south-eastern Europe to Hungary, as well as including most of North Africa. The Ottomans threatened to expand into Western Europe, but in both 1529 and 1683 were turned back after defeats at Vienna. In Ottoman territories in the Balkans and Greece they carried out a policy known as *devshirme* (which literally means 'collecting'), where Christian boys were taken from their families, forcibly converted to Islam, and trained as soldiers and civil servants – this continued until the mid-seventeenth century. The most talented were recruited as janissaries, the elite bodyguard of the sultan. Similarly, thousands of Christian girls were abducted and sold into sexual slavery – some ended up in the Imperial Harem, where a handful rose to prominence as concubines or mothers of the sultan.

fostered a spirit of progress, liberty and tolerance. At its heart lay reason – many optimistically hoped that rational thought and reform could conquer all. A crucial aspect of the Enlightenment was the creation of a 'public sphere' – spaces outside the control of higher authorities like the Church and state (for example, coffee houses, salons and learned societies) where anyone who wanted to could debate and discuss matters freely. There was a trend towards scepticism about religion. Some philosophers began to question fundamental tenets of religion. Deism (the belief in God but not organized religion) became more common, although outright atheism was rare.

France was the heart of the Enlightenment, and home to many of its key figures, who were known as the *philosophes*. One of the most important was Baron de Montesquieu (1689–1755), a radical whose *Spirit of the Laws* (1748) proposed sweeping changes in government, including constitutions, laws to ensure liberty, and the separation of powers. The Enlightenment saw a search for universal knowledge and laws, inspiring the creation of the *Encyclopédie*. This was an ambitious project co-edited by two men: Denis Diderot (1713–84) and Jean le Rond d'Alembert (1717–83). Diderot was a philosopher who constantly struggled with financial problems and d'Alembert was a mathematician, named after the Parisian church where he had been left as an infant. For their project they commissioned thousands of articles from the greatest thinkers of the day (including themselves), as well as hundreds of illustrations. The first volume of the *Encyclopédie* was published in 1751. By 1772 it had run to twenty-eight volumes, with a total of 71,818 articles.

The most famous figure of the Enlightenment was Voltaire (1694–1778), a wildly prolific writer and philosopher born François-Marie Arouet in Paris. His controversial writing led to him being imprisoned for eleven months in the Bastille and exiled to London from 1726 to 1728. After being allowed to return home, he joined a scheme that took advantage of a loophole in the French state lottery, winning him a fortune.

Financially secure, he continued to ridicule traditional French government, religion and society, which meant he was often banned from Paris. His most famous work, *Candide* (1759), satirized the optimistic view that we live in the best of all possible worlds.

Another major thinker was Jean-Jacques Rousseau (1712–78), who was born in Geneva but spent much of his life in Paris. His *Discourse on Inequality*, written in 1754, argued that property had caused inequality and humans lived in a perfect state of nature before being corrupted. In 1762 Rousseau published *The Social Contract*, which argued sovereignty should be in the hands of the people rather than monarchs. Rousseau's works were controversial and often banned, but nonetheless he became hugely influential on the development of political thought and the French Revolution.

In Germany the Enlightenment was known as the *Aufklärung*. It saw the promotion of German language and culture. During the later eighteenth century, the *Sturm und Drang* ('storm and stress') movement emerged. It rejected the rationality of the earlier Enlightenment, calling for people to be subjective and give their emotion freer reign. Central to this spirit were the writers Johann Wolfgang von Goethe (1749–1832) and Friedrich Schiller (1759–1805). Another German to question many core Enlightenment values was the philosopher Immanual Kant (1724–1804), who argued that reason alone was not enough to understand everything. As the eighteenth century ended, Romanticism became more popular and influential across Europe. It stressed emotion, imagination and spontaneity, and led to more interest in nature and folklore.

Enlightened Absolutists

During the eighteenth century, some European monarchs, influenced by the Enlightenment, began to reform their nations through their autocratic power. This trend varied between different countries but generally emphasized codification of laws, religious tolerance, promotion of trade, and limiting the power of Church and nobility.

In Prussia, a kingdom that covered much of modern-day Germany and parts of Poland, Frederick II (1712–86) was the enlightened absolutist *par excellence*. His predecessors had laid the foundations for a bureaucratic state with a strong military. Frederick came to the throne in 1740 and reformed his kingdom. He increased Prussia's wealth by encouraging skilled workers to migrate there, regardless of their religion. He was also a patron of the arts and learning, and the Prussian Academy of Sciences in Berlin became one of Europe's intellectual centres. In addition, Frederick was a great general who transformed Prussia into a major power. During the 1740s, he conquered the region of Silesia from the Austrian Habsburgs. In 1756 Austria allied with France in an attempt to win back Silesia. This contributed to the outbreak of the Seven Years' War (1756–63), which drew in all of Europe and spread out to Asia, Africa and the Americas, making it the first global conflict. Prussia (with British support) retained control of Silesia.

Prussia's southern neighbour, Austria, had its own enlightened monarch: Maria Theresa (1717–80). She was the only child of Holy Roman Emperor Charles VI (1685–1740) and, as a woman, she was unable to inherit his imperial title.

Charles wanted to ensure she would inherit his Austrian realms, and issued an edict called the 'Pragmatic Sanction' in order to allow this. Nevertheless, when Maria Theresa came to the throne she faced the War of the Austrian Succession (1740–8), in which she and her allies fought to keep her inheritance. She lost Silesia to Prussia, and Parma in northern Italy to Spain, but otherwise kept most of her patrimony. Maria Theresa's husband, Francis I (1708–65), became Holy Roman Emperor, but had little role in government. She held the real power in Austria and transformed it from a weak, indebted state to an increasingly powerful and centralized one with an effective taxation system. She introduced a new civil and criminal code and reformed the Church and education system. In some respects Maria Theresa was deeply conservative, particularly regarding religious toleration of her non-Catholic subjects.

The later eighteenth century saw another woman rise to rule a European power: Catherine the Great (1729–96) of Russia. She was a German noblewoman who in 1745 married Peter the Great's grandson Peter III (1728–62). They grew to despise each other. After Peter came to the throne in 1762, Catherine organized a coup against him, which overthrew him after 186 days and installed her on the throne. Mindful of the conservatism of many in Russia, Catherine instituted a regime of gradual reform. She revised the law code, fully secularized Church lands and limited the clergy's power. She established the Hermitage Museum and hundreds of state institutions that educated boys and girls.

The leading enlightened monarch in the Mediterranean was Charles III of Spain (1716–88), who also ruled Naples and Sicily from 1734 to 1759. In southern Italy he had created a commercial council to build up the economy and patronized the arts and learning by building an opera house, founding an academy and museum, and encouraging excavations of the ruins of Pompeii. After his half-brother Ferdinand VI of Spain (1713–59) died childless, Charles travelled across the Mediterranean to succeed him there (leaving his Italian lands to his younger son). Charles was determined to reform Spain, which had regressed since its golden age in the sixteenth century. He limited the influence of the Church by reducing the powers of the Inquisition and expelling the Jesuits. Economically, he abolished laws that restricted trade, built roads and canals, and established royal factories. Charles also sought to make Spain a true nation, rather than a collection of separate provinces, by establishing its national anthem in 1770 and flag in 1785.

Enlightened absolutism was not just associated with monarchs: in Portugal its policies were carried out by the chief minister to Joseph I (1714–77), the Marquis of Pombal (1699–1782). His greatest achievement was organizing the recovery after the Lisbon Earthquake of 1755. This was the strongest seismic event in recorded European history, and caused a huge tsunami. The city suffered 50,000 dead and 85 per cent of it was destroyed. Pombal took swift steps to stop the spread of disorder and disease and helped design a new city. He ensured it would be earthquake-proof by getting soldiers to march around scale models to simulate the impact of a future seismic event.

In Denmark, enlightened reforms were carried out by a German doctor, Johann Friedrich Struensee (1737–72), physician to Christian VII (1749–1808). Christian suffered from severe mental illness, which meant that from 1770 to 1772 Struensee (who was also having an affair with the queen) took over control of the government. He attempted to radically reform Denmark but was overthrown by a conservative coup and executed.

CHAPTER 4

THE AGE OF
REVOLUTIONS

THE FIRST INDUSTRIAL REVOLUTION

For the vast bulk of European (and indeed global) history,
economic growth was slow. This changed as a result of
the Industrial Revolution, a transition to a new way of
manufacturing. Instead of relying on the muscle-power of
animals and humans (often supplemented by wind), it made
use of mechanical sources of energy driven first by water,
then steam. This First Industrial Revolution began in Britain
from the mid-eighteenth century, before spreading into the
rest of Europe over the first half of the nineteenth century.

The textile industry was the first to be fully mechanized.
This began in Britain, where wages were higher than the rest
of Europe, encouraging investment in labour-saving devices.
These had to be housed in mills, which developed into the first
factories. Over time, other industries (such as shoemaking
and metalwork) adopted this mode of production. Other
European economies were slower to mechanize because their
lower wages meant they had no impetus to invest in new
technologies. From around 1800, British innovations began
to be introduced on the Continent; first in Belgium, then

in France, Switzerland and Germany. The building block of the Industrial Revolution was iron ore. This was smelted into wrought iron, which had a vast range of applications, from tools to machinery to construction (the Eiffel Tower was made using it). As with textiles, processes that made cheaper and higher-quality wrought iron possible were first invented in Britain.

Steam power was also vital. The earliest steam engines were developed in Britain in the eighteenth century. At first used to pump water, they were improved so they could drive machinery. These devices were powered by burning coal, which generated energy more cheaply and efficiently than wood or peat. Although British coal was initially dominant, deposits were found and mined in other countries, particularly France, Belgium, Germany, Poland and Russia.

The Industrial Revolution was accompanied by urbanization, with rural populations shifting to towns and cities. At the same time, there was rapid population growth; people began to marry earlier and have more children, while mortality levels slowly decreased. This meant Europe's population rose from around 100 million in 1700 to nearly 500 million in 1900.

THE FRENCH REVOLUTION

The French king wielded absolute power, with government centralized in his person. By the later eighteenth century such absolutism was out of date, particularly after Louis XVI (1754–93) came to the throne in 1774. He was conservative and indecisive; unsuited to the challenges his regime faced. His

Austrian wife, Marie Antoinette (1755–93), became deeply unpopular due to her nationality and lavish spending.

By the 1780s France was in financial crisis. Its support for the Americans during their war for independence from Britain had left the country heavily indebted. In 1788 France suspended payment to its creditors – it was bankrupt. To find a solution, Louis summoned the Estates General. This was an assembly of the three estates (clergy, nobility and commoners) that had not sat together since 1614. It opened in Versailles in May 1789, but quickly fractured. In June the Commons declared itself a National Assembly, and vowed not to dissolve until it had written a new constitution. By the end of the month, it was joined by the other two estates to form the National Constituent Assembly, which would help govern and draft a constitution.

Political clubs opened across France. The most important was the Jacobins, which grew to 500,000 members. Censorship broke down, enabling the spread of radical ideas. Some called for the abolition of the monarchy and its replacement with a republic. In summer 1789, public order disintegrated due to rising food prices and low wages. On 14 July a crowd stormed the Bastille Prison in Paris, symbolizing the end of the old order (even though they only freed a handful of people). In October a mob, led by women protesting the price of bread, marched on Versailles and forced the royal family to move to the Tuileries Palace in Paris. There was an uneasy equilibrium until June 1791, when the royal family fled Paris to join Royalist forces in north-eastern France and initiate a counter-revolution. They were discovered en route and forced to return. This exacerbated fears Louis could not be trusted, and increased support for a republic. Louis was forced to accept a constitution that created an elected Legislative Assembly, which gathered for the first time on 1 October.

Other European powers looked on fearfully, concerned radicalism might spread. Austria and Prussia threatened retribution if Louis was harmed. In April 1792, war broke out, initially going badly for France. The foreign threat radicalized Paris and led to the summoning of a National Convention elected by all men over twenty-five. The tide turned when the invaders were defeated at the Battle of Valmy on 20 September. Emboldened, the National Convention abolished royalty and declared France a republic. Louis was stripped of his titles and tried for treason – he was guillotined on 21 January 1793 (Marie Antoinette followed that October).

Louis' execution united Europe against France, with Britain, Spain, the Netherlands, Portugal and Naples all joining the coalition against it. There was armed internal opposition from Royalists – particularly in the Vendée region in west-central France. In March 1793, the Committee of Public Safety took the reins of executive government. It was led by the radical Jacobin Maximilien Robespierre (1758–94), who vowed to safeguard the revolution whatever the cost. This led to the Reign of Terror that started in September. All potential enemies of the revolution were subject to arrest, imprisonment or execution. Over 17,500 were killed and 250,000 imprisoned. The new regime introduced a new decimal calendar, with Year I starting on 22 September 1792. Robespierre introduced a new deist state religion, the Cult of the Supreme Being, to replace Catholicism. The Reign of Terror ended in July 1794, when moderates in the National

Convention turned against Robespierre and executed him and his allies before abolishing most of his reforms.

A new, more conservative, constitution was passed in 1795. France was led by the Directory, a group of three selected by an elected legislature. The Directory failed to bring stability to war torn France, and lost popular support. In 1799 the young general Napoleon Bonaparte (1769–1821) seized power in a coup. France was to be ruled by a three-man consulate headed by Napoleon, who had dictatorial powers. The French Revolution was over and the Napoleonic regime had begun.

THE SPIRIT OF REVOLUTION

Political upheaval swept Europe in the later eighteenth century. The first of these revolutions occurred in Corsica, which had been annexed by Genoa in 1347. In 1755 Pasquale Paoli (1725–1807) declared the independent Corsican Republic, and drove the Genoese off the island. The Corsican Constitution gave the vote to all men over twenty-five (some women also voted). Genoa sold its claim on Corsica to France and in 1768 the French launched an invasion, defeating Paoli's republican forces. Corsica then became a French province. France was also involved in anti-revolutionary activity in Geneva. The city was divided between a dominant pro-French elite and republican populists. In 1782 crowds supportive of the populists helped them seize control. France sent in soldiers to repress the democratic movement, and restored traditional elites to power.

Although the Netherlands was technically a republic, a hereditary office called the Stadtholder held by the Princes of Orange wielded significant power. By the later eighteenth century, it effectively served as a monarchy. A republican movement called the Patriots wanted to reduce the power of the Stadtholder, William V (1748–1806), and create a democratic republic. The Patriots formed militias called the Free Corps across the country. From 1785 the Patriots used their military strength to force elections of new officials in towns. William's power dwindled away. His rule was restored in autumn 1787 thanks to the military intervention of his brother-in-law Frederick William II of Prussia (1744–97).

There was often populist reaction against centralizing monarchs. None overstepped traditional boundaries further than Joseph II (1741–90). He had been Holy Roman Emperor since 1765 but was excluded from governing Austria and the Habsburg realms by his mother, Maria Theresa, until her death in 1780. When Joseph finally wielded power, he embarked on a series of radical reforms, ignoring all warnings of caution. He issued six thousand edicts and eleven thousand laws. Joseph secularized Church lands, granted toleration to Protestants and Jews, abolished the death penalty and ended censorship. He wanted to bring together the diverse components of his realm by centralizing power; he limited the strength of regional assemblies in Hungary, Milan and the Austrian Netherlands (modern-day Belgium) and made German the official language everywhere. Nobles grew to despise him, forcing him to abandon his attempts to abolish serfdom, and commoners bridled against his constant interference. By 1790 there was unrest across his realms. With his regime under threat, Joseph cancelled almost all of his reforms, and died less than a month later.

The strongest reaction against Joseph was in the Austrian Netherlands. The Brabant Revolution began in 1789 as a protest against Joseph, and evolved into an independence movement. After rebel forces defeated an Austrian army at the Battle of Turnhout, there was a national uprising, and on 20 December independence was declared, with an independent republic called the United Belgian States being established on 11 January 1790. At the same time there was a revolt in Liège, where the ruling Prince-Bishop was overthrown and a republic declared. These new regimes did not last. In summer 1790, the Austrians regrouped and sent in troops who by the end of the year had re-established control and restored Habsburg rule in Belgium. In January 1791, the Austrians entered Liège and restored the Prince-Bishop.

Notable Europeans: Tadeusz Kósciuszko (1774–1817)

The revolutionary spirit spread to Poland. In 1772 the Polish-Lithuanian Commonwealth had dwindled in size when Austria, Russia and Prussia annexed some of its territory. Traditionally, the powers of the King of Poland were limited because nobles had extensive privileges. They not only elected the king but also controlled the Sejm, an assembly that had power of veto. In 1791 a Polish constitution was declared with the support of King Stanisław II Augustus (1732–98). It created a democratic system of constitutional monarchy, limited noble power and gave serfs greater legal protection. Russia opposed the constitution, as it believed it would make the Polish monarch too strong, and invaded in 1792. With the support of conservative Polish nobles, the Russians forced Stanisław to surrender. The next year Prussia and Russia claimed even more Polish territory. As a result, a Polish general called Tadeusz Kościuszko, who had fought for the Americans during the Revolutionary War, led an uprising against Russian rule. He called for the abolition of serfdom and for universal civil liberties. From 1794 to 1795 he was defeated, and the remaining Polish territory was carved up. Poland was wiped from the map, and would not re-emerge as an independent state until 1918.

Notable Europeans: Napoleon (1769–1821)

Napoleon Bonaparte was born in Corsica, the son of a local nobleman. In 1785 he entered the French Army as a junior artillery officer, and rose through the ranks during the nascent Republic's struggle to survive. Napoleon became a prominent figure in 1795, when he held off a Royalist attempt to take Paris. Hailed as a hero, he was given command of a French army that was invading Italy. The influence of Napoleon's lover (and later wife) Joséphine de Beauharnais (1763–1814), mistress to several leading politicians, was also vital in helping him win promotion.

The Italian Campaign was a triumph – Napoleon won a series of victories and in 1797 forced Austria to make peace, ending the War of the First Coalition. Napoleon's first failure was during the War of the Second Coalition in his Egyptian campaign – after invading in 1798, French forces failed to maintain control of the region. Napoleon had returned home

The Napoleonic Empire, *c.* 1810

in late 1799, seizing power and naming himself First Consul. He consolidated his position with victory over the Austrians at Marengo in northern Italy in 1800. Hostilities were ended when peace was made with Britain in 1802.

For all of his military triumphs, Napoleon regarded his greatest triumph as the reform of the French legal system. In March 1804, the Napoleonic Code came into force, replacing France's outdated patchwork of customs and laws. For the first time France had a single, clearly written, legal code. It granted freedom of religion and forbade privileges based on birth. Napoleon created a society where it was service to him that brought status, rather than social rank.

In November 1804, Napoleon promulgated a new constitution that made him Emperor of the French. The House of Bonaparte was established as an imperial dynasty. He also created 'family kingdoms' for his relatives in Naples, the Netherlands, Westphalia, Spain and Tuscany. They were vassal states with little independence. Napoleon still lacked an heir, so in 1810 he divorced Joséphine and married Marie Louise (1791–1847), the daughter of the Austrian emperor. She gave birth to a son in 1811. However, for all of its successes Napoleon's regime would unravel as a result of his imperialist schemes.

THE NAPOLEONIC WARS

After the French Revolution, Europe was plunged into a period of warfare that lasted from 1792 to 1815. France faced several coalitions, with Britain emerging as its most formidable opponent. Fearing Napoleon's ambitions, Britain declared war in 1803, beginning the War of the Third Coalition. Napoleon wanted to invade Britain but was unable to gain the naval dominance he needed to ferry his army across the Channel. When Austria and Russia joined the anti-French alliance, Napoleon marched east. He won a great victory over an Austrian-Russian army at Austerlitz in December 1805. Austria was forced to surrender, while the Russians retreated. The war at sea was less successful. At

Trafalgar, in October 1805, the British navy had destroyed a Franco-Spanish fleet. For the rest of the wars France would never match Britain's maritime strength.

In 1806 Napoleon created the Confederation of the Rhine, a string of German states that recognized him as their protector. This ended the Holy Roman Empire. The Confederation was a threat to Prussia, which went to war with Napoleon in August that year, beginning the War of the Fourth Coalition. Prussia was exposed because its main ally, Russia, had not yet mobilized. Napoleon advanced into Prussia and captured Berlin. The next year he defeated Russia, but he still needed to best Britain. Unable to invade, in 1806 he declared a trade embargo, hoping it would undermine the British economy. He demanded all European nations join his 'Continental System'. The policy was impossible to enforce and smuggling was rife. When Portugal refused to join, France invaded in 1807 and forced its royal family into exile. Napoleon then conquered Spain, deposing its king and installing his brother Joseph Bonaparte (1768–1844) in 1808. This led to a nationwide uprising and the Peninsular War. Spain and Portugal, aided by British reinforcements and supplies, successfully fought for liberation in a bitter conflict that lasted until 1814.

In 1809 Austria attacked Napoleon, beginning the War of the Fifth Coalition. In just seven months the Austrians were defeated, leaving Napoleon at the height of his power. In 1812 he took the decision that led to his downfall. As Russia had refused to adhere to the Continental System, he invaded with nearly half a million men. The Russians adopted a scorched-earth policy, destroying anything that could help the invader. Napoleon fought his way to Moscow. However, with his supply lines stretched and Russia defiant, he ordered a retreat in mid-October. The march was a bitter and slow one; soldiers lacked warm clothes and supplies, and suffered constant attack by Russian light cavalry. By the time Napoleon's forces left Russian territory they had lost around 80 per cent of their original number due to casualties, desertion and disease.

The Russian debacle gave succour to Napoleon's enemies, who formed a grand alliance against him. In the War of the Sixth Coalition, which began in 1813, Napoleon lost control of Germany, and in early 1814 coalition forces entered France. Napoleon, unable to retain the support of his generals and the French people, abdicated on 11 April. Louis XVIII (1755–1824), brother of Louis XVI, returned from exile in England to rule as a constitutional monarch.

Napoleon was confined to the Mediterranean island of Elba but escaped in February 1815. After landing in France, he marched on Paris, accompanied by soldiers who flocked to his banner, and reclaimed power. Britain, Russia, Austria and Prussia vowed to put 150,000 men each into the field to defeat him. On 18 June, Napoleon met a British-Prussian army at Waterloo. His army was routed and Napoleon abdicated for the second time. He was exiled to the remote Atlantic island of St Helena, where he died in 1821.

The make-up of post-war Europe was decided at the Congress of Vienna, which met from November 1814 to June 1815. The decisions made were largely conservative, aimed at opposing revolutionary and nationalist sentiment. Vienna created a diplomatic mechanism to keep peace, the 'Concert of Europe', which helped prevent major war between Europe's great powers for nearly four decades.

GERMAN UNIFICATION

The Holy Roman Empire was ultimately replaced by the German Confederation, a federation of thirty-nine states, each of which retained a great deal of independence. The leading power was Austria, which sought to maintain the status quo. The Austrian chief minister, Klemens von Metternich (1773–1859), was a conservative determined to prevent nationalism becoming a political force. This ran against the tide of pan-Germanism, which aimed to bring together all of the German-speaking peoples. There was tension between Austria and Prussia, the two largest powers in the Confederation, particularly over economic matters. Prussia was the main proponent of the Zollverein, a customs union established in 1834, which created a free-trade zone in the Confederation. By 1842 most German states had joined. They did not include Austria because Metternich opposed the idea, as he wanted to protect domestic industry from foreign competition.

In 1848, during the Spring of Nations, people across the Confederation demanded an end to autocracy in a movement called the March Revolution. Crowds in Berlin forced the King of Prussia, Frederick William IV (1795–1861), to grant elections, a constitution, and pledge his support for German unification. There was disorder in Bavaria, the third-largest state in the Confederation. Its king, Ludwig I (1786–1868), had a scandalous open relationship with his mistress Lola Montez (1821–61), an Irish dancer born Eliza Rosanna Gilbert. Montez had tried to use her influence on Ludwig to make him pass liberal reforms, leading to conservatives taking to the streets to demand her removal. They were opposed by liberal students. Unwilling to give up any powers, Ludwig abdicated in favour of his son, who oversaw moderate reforms. Montez fled to Switzerland, and spent the rest of her life travelling the world as an entertainer and public speaker.

The protests led to the German people being allowed to elect a national parliament, which assembled in Frankfurt in May. The Frankfurt Parliament proclaimed a German Empire that would have Frederick William as its constitutional monarch. He declined, saying he would not accept a 'crown from the gutter'. The Confederation staggered on, but it had been fatally weakened. The man who delivered the death blow was Otto von Bismarck (1815–98), who became prime minister of Prussia in 1862. He was determined to unify Germany under Prussian leadership. Prussia's army was reorganized and modernized; in 1864 it defeated Denmark, and the Danes were forced to give up the disputed territory of Schleswig-Holstein. Two years later Prussia prevailed over Austria in a six-week war, ending Austrian influence over German affairs. This led to the dissolution of the German Confederation. It was replaced by the North German Confederation, a Prussian-led alliance from which Austria was excluded.

Bismarck's next master stroke was to manoeuvre France into declaring war on Prussia in 1870. He predicted that the conflict would unite German states behind Prussia. France was swiftly defeated. On 18 January 1871, the Prussian king was declared Kaiser Wilhelm I (1797–1888), ruler of the German Empire, which was a federation of twenty-five states with Prussia the dominant force. The kaiser had wide powers including control of foreign policy and appointment of the federal chancellor (Bismarck was given the office), but there was also an elected legislative assembly, the Reichstag. This German Empire became a major power, and by the end of the century was Europe's largest economy.

THE RISORGIMENTO

Italy had been fragmented since the sixth century. During the early nineteenth century, a movement in support of unification arose, the *Risorgimento* ('Resurgence'). Many opposed this, notably the Austrians, who ruled much of northern Italy. Secret societies that favoured unification and democracy were formed across Italy. The largest were the Carbonari, who in 1820 led a revolt in Naples that the Austrians suppressed. From 1830 to 1831, the Carbonari were involved in revolts in Parma, Modena and the Papal States. Austria used military force to quash them, leading many to renounce revolutionary activity. One man refused to countenance retreat: Giuseppe Mazzini (1805–72), a journalist and Carbonari member who went into exile in Marseille, where he formed a group called Young Italy. He wanted to rally the Italian people together to create a united republic liberated from Austrian influence. Mazzini's most important ally was Giuseppe Garibaldi (1807–82), who became the military figurehead of Italian independence.

The year 1848 was a watershed in Italian history. In the Kingdom of Sardinia (which also ruled most of north-western Italy), Charles Albert (1798–1849) proclaimed a liberal constitution that granted a free press and gave his subjects the right to elect a legislative assembly. He and his successors emerged as the main opponents of Austrian involvement in Italy and supporters of some form of unification. Elsewhere, an uprising in Palermo escalated into a revolution in Sicily and Naples (together known as the Kingdom of the Two Sicilies). In March there was an insurrection against Austria in Veneto in north-eastern Italy, which joined Sardinia. Revolt then spread to Lombardy, forcing the Austrians to withdraw. The pope fled Rome and a short-lived republic was declared there until French support allowed the resumption of papal rule. The Austrians rebounded and reconquered Veneto before defeating the Sardinians in 1849, forcing Charles Albert to abdicate. This First Italian War of Independence ended with revolutionary forces seemingly crushed.

After this setback, the Count of Cavour (1810–61), prime minister of Sardinia, emerged as the architect of Italian unification. It would not be a republic but a monarchy under the new King of Sardinia, Victor Emmanuel II (1820–78). Cavour used diplomacy to gain the support of other powers for his policies. The Second Italian War of Independence saw Sardinia (with French support) annex Lombardy in 1859. The next year they added Parma, Modena, Tuscany and the Papal States (excluding the area around Rome). In the Kingdom of the Two Sicilies, Garibaldi led a volunteer army that overthrew the monarchy there. Southern Italy and Sicily then joined the north. In 1861 Victor Emmanuel proclaimed himself King of Italy, naming Cavour as its first prime minister. The Austrians still controlled Veneto, but in 1866 it was conquered (with Prussian support) after the Third Italian War of Independence. Rome was annexed in 1870, completing the *Risorgimento*.

The Decline of the Ottoman Empire

Ottoman power had waned in the face of territorial losses, internal conflict, weak rulers and ineffective government. In the Balkans, which had been mostly under Ottoman sovereignty since the fourteenth century, there was a rising tide of nationalist sentiment. The first place to revolt was Serbia, in 1804. After thirteen years of warfare Serbia became a fully autonomous principality. In subsequent decades, the Ottomans faced uprisings across the Balkans. By 1875 most of the region was in open rebellion. Other European powers, led by Russia, intervened. Under the 1878 Treaty of Berlin, the Ottomans were forced to recognize the complete independence of Serbia, Romania and Montenegro, as well as the autonomy of Bulgaria (which declared itself independent in 1908).

On the domestic front, the sultans attempted to modernize and reform but faced serious financial difficulties. In 1876 Abdul Hamid II (1842–1918) came to the throne. One of his first acts was to promulgate a constitution, but two years later he suspended it and ruled as an autocrat. Abdul Hamid suppressed liberal activism and violently persecuted minorities, particularly the Armenians. In 1908 the Young Turk Revolution, a movement of reformist groups, led to the restoration of the constitution. The next year Abdul Hamid was overthrown and replaced by his brother Mehmed V (1844–1918), a figurehead with no real power. The Ottoman Empire continued to lose territory (including Bosnia-Herzegovina to Austria-Hungary) and remained prone to instability.

GREEK INDEPENDENCE

The Ottomans had ruled Greece since the mid-fifteenth century. The Greeks also agitated for independence, and the country revolted in 1821. Many in Europe were sympathetic to the Greeks, particularly the Russians because of their shared Christian Orthodox faith. Foreigners volunteered for the Greek cause, including the English romantic poet Lord Byron (1788–1824), who died of a fever while fighting the Ottomans. In 1827 Russia, Britain and France intervened; sending a fleet that destroyed the Ottoman navy at the Battle of Navarino in the Ionian Sea. The Ottomans were forced to recognize Greek independence in 1832. A German prince, Otto of Bavaria (1815–67), was selected as monarch for the new Kingdom of Greece. He tried at first to be an absolute monarch but in 1843 was forced to accede to a constitution. Other Greek-speaking parts of the Ottoman Empire gradually split off and joined Greece.

FRANCE'S STRUGGLE FOR STABILITY

After the Napoleonic Wars, the victorious powers had reduced France to its 1790 borders, levied reparations of 700 million francs, and imposed an occupying army of 150,000 (withdrawn in 1818). The Bourbon Dynasty was restored, placing Louis XVIII on the French throne. He ruled as a constitutional monarch, and left many duties to his ministers.

Not wishing to divide France, he did not pursue vengeance against former revolutionaries or Bonapartists and tried to limit the influence of the 'Ultras', Royalists who favoured a return to absolute monarchy.

After Louis died childless in 1824, his younger brother Charles X (1757–1836) succeeded him. Charles favoured Ultras, gave more power to the Church and quarrelled with liberals. He lost public support, but Charles would not forgo his reactionary policies. In July 1830 he issued a set of repressive new laws. The people of Paris had had enough – in the three-day July Revolution they rose up and forced Charles to flee the country. The French throne was declared vacant by the provisional government. On 9 August a new king was declared: Louis Philippe, Duke of Orléans (1773–1850). He was Charles' distant cousin and openly favoured the liberal opposition; in the past he had supported the Revolution and even been a member of the Jacobins. He was proclaimed 'King of the French' and restored the *Tricolore* as the national flag in place of the white Bourbon banner. Known as the 'Citizen King', he accepted a new constitution that reduced royal powers.

As Louis Philippe aged, he became less liberal and attempted to stifle those who called for further reform. In February 1848, Parisians took to the streets in protest. Louis Philippe was unable to prevent the disorder; his government collapsed and he fled to England, where he died in 1850. The Second French Republic was declared, with universal male suffrage. The head of state was a directly elected president limited to a single four-year term. The victor in the presidential elections was Louis-Napoleon Bonaparte (1808–73), nephew of the late emperor. In 1851, with his term running down, Louis-Napoleon staged a coup that dissolved parliament and extended his powers and term. The next year he went even further: he proclaimed the Second French Empire and on 2 December 1852 (forty-eight years to the day after his uncle's coronation) he declared himself Emperor Napoleon III, with authoritarian powers. His regime oversaw industrialization and the expansion of the French colonial empire in Africa, Asia and Oceania.

Napoleon III's reign ended as a result of his decision to go to war with Prussia in 1870. French forces were outmatched by the Prussians, who enjoyed a technological and numerical advantage. The Prussians and their German allies advanced into north-eastern France and at the Battle of Sedan encircled the main French army. Napoleon III, who was accompanying his forces, surrendered himself to the Prussians and, following a few months' captivity in Germany, died in exile in England. After Sedan the Third French Republic was declared. The new regime continued the war, but surrendered in January 1871 after the Prussians laid siege to, and briefly occupied, Paris. That March there was an uprising in Paris, as radicals seized control of the city. The Paris Commune lasted for two months, until government forces recaptured the city after a week of street-to-street combat. After this upheaval, the Third Republic established a functioning, mostly stable, democracy.

THE BELGIAN REVOLUTION

After the Napoleonic Wars, Belgium and the Netherlands were united into a kingdom ruled by the Prince of Orange, who became King William I (1772–1843). He was unpopular in Belgium because he imposed the Dutch language on the government and education system. This, combined with economic recession and the July Revolution in France, led to unrest in Belgium. On 25 August 1830, there was an uprising in Brussels after a performance of the opera *The Mute Girl of Portici*, which featured a patriotic song that caused crowds to flock into the streets. They chanted patriotic slogans and seized government buildings. When William sent in eight thousand Dutch soldiers, it led to a general uprising. On 4 October Belgian independence was declared. It was recognized by Europe's great powers at the London Conference that December, where they signed a treaty permanently guaranteeing Belgian independence. Independent Belgium was a constitutional monarchy, and first offered its throne to Louis Philippe's second son. He rejected the offer, so the Belgians turned to a German noble, Leopold of Saxe-Coburg and Gotha (1790–1865). His descendants still reign as monarchs of the Belgians. Likewise, William's lineage continues to occupy the Dutch throne.

The Spring of Nations

In 1848 a wave of revolutions swept across Europe. They were largely liberal, aiming to create democratic, independent nation-states. Protests spread to over fifty states, although they did not have a great impact in Russia, Britain, the Low Countries and the Iberian Peninsula. Common demands included a constitution, greater democratic rights, and freedom of the press. There was a wide base of support for reform, with the bourgeoisie, rural peasants and urban workers allying together.

The opening salvo was fired in January. It was a revolt in Sicily against the ruling Bourbon dynasty. The rebels won independence – but it only lasted sixteen months before the Bourbons re-established themselves. In northern Italy there were unsuccessful protests against Austrian rule. As has been discussed earlier, there was also the February Revolution in France that led to the overthrow of Louis Philippe I and the short-lived Second French Republic. In March there was a series of protests across Germany that called for democracy and national unity.

Nationalism was an increasingly powerful force in nineteenth-century Europe. As such, the Austrian Empire, which was a patchwork of different ethnicities and languages, was primed for nationalist revolutions demanding autonomy or independence. The most important was the Hungarian Revolution, where demonstrators made a series of demands including an independent national parliament and army, equality before the law, and an end to censorship. This forced the resignation of Metternich, who had been imperial chancellor since 1821. Although Emperor Ferdinand I (1793–1875) agreed to the demands of the Hungarian revolutionaries, the protests escalated into a war of independence. Ferdinand was unable to provide strong leadership; he suffered from a range of ailments including epilepsy and a speech impediment, and left most of his official duties to his counsellors. In December he abdicated in favour of his nephew Franz Joseph I (1830–1916). A reactionary, Franz Joseph restored Habsburg control of Hungary by calling on the assistance of the Russians, who helped him crush the revolutionaries. In the long term, a compromise was reached in 1867, which established the dual monarchy of Austria-Hungary. Hungary had its own parliament but no control over foreign policy, and Franz Joseph remained head of state.

Scandinavia showed the mixed success of the revolutions. In Sweden (which was joined in union with Norway under a single monarch until 1905) there was rioting in Stockholm but it was quickly suppressed. In neighbouring Denmark, King Frederick VII (1808–63) acceded to the demands of reformers, gave up his absolute powers and accepted a constitution that meant the monarchy would share power with an elected parliament. As such, Denmark was something of an outlier because its revolution was both peaceful and successful. In 1848 most places in Europe echoed events in Sweden, with traditional authorities able to hold on to power following a burst of upheaval. However, the Spring of Nations left an important legacy, as over subsequent decades many European regimes would adopt programmes of gradual reform to forestall future disorder.

THE CRIMEAN WAR

As the Ottoman Empire declined, Russia extended its influence at the ailing power's expense. In October 1853, war broke out between Russia and the Ottomans over control of Moldavia and Wallachia. Europe's great powers wanted to use diplomatic means to solve the dispute, but both Britain and France grew concerned that a Russian victory would threaten their positions in the eastern Mediterranean and Asia. Russia's destruction of an Ottoman fleet at Sinope, on the southern coast of the Black Sea, exacerbated Anglo-French fears. In March 1854, Britain and France declared war on Russia. As fighting between Russia and the Ottomans raged in Eastern Europe and the Caucasus, French and British forces were sent into the Black Sea, with the aim of capturing Sevastopol, a heavily fortified Russian city and naval base in Crimea. The Siege of Sevastopol began in October 1854 and displayed the savagery of industrialized warfare. Newly developed rifles and heavy artillery caused devastating injuries, and the siege devolved into trench warfare that prefigured the conditions of the First World War. The British and French found supplying their forces problematic – combined with a cold winter and unhygienic conditions, it meant diseases like typhus and cholera became endemic. The siege ended in September 1855, when the Russians withdrew from Sevastopol. This contributed to Russia suing for peace in March 1856, leading to the Treaty of Paris that ended the war. The war did not halt the decline of the Ottoman Empire, and rising nationalist sentiment within it.

Reform and Revolution in Russia

The Crimean War persuaded many in Russia that modernization was vital. Alexander II (1818–81) agreed. He passed a range of reforms, including the momentous step of abolishing serfdom in 1861. Peasants were no longer the property of their landlords. However, former serfs were forced to pay 'redemption' debts to their former owners and were still constrained to their village community. Radicals did not believe Alexander II was moving quickly enough. Revolutionary groups sprang up, some of them willing to use violence. One of them, People's Will, targeted government officials for assassination. No one was safe, not even the emperor. In 1881 two members of People's Will threw bombs at the imperial carriage as it travelled through St Petersburg. Alexander II survived the first blast but the second tore him apart. Ironically, Alexander II had been on the verge of accepting moderate reforms that would have laid the foundations for constitutional monarchy. His son and successor, Alexander III (1845–94), refused to countenance any reductions to his autocratic power and reversed many of his father's policies.

The Jewish population of the Russian Empire had long been the target of prejudice and violence. Following Alexander II's assassination there were pogroms across the empire, as rioting crowds attacked Jewish neighbourhoods. In 1882 the government passed the first of several anti-semitic laws that placed legal restrictions on the Jewish population. Pogroms continued, with the government doing little to stop them (and in some cases helping to organize the violence). Around 2 million Jews emigrated from the Russian Empire between 1881 and 1920.

After Alexander III died of kidney disease in 1894, his son Nicholas II (1868–1918) succeeded him. He combined his father's reactionary attitudes with narrow-mindedness and incompetence. Seeking to extend its sphere of influence into Korea and Manchuria, Russia was drawn into war with Japan in February 1904. Nicholas and his advisors believed they would win a swift victory. Against these arrogant expectations, Japan defeated Russia after eighteen months of fighting. Things went badly for Nicholas on the domestic front. Socialist and Marxist ideas were growing influential among Russia's urban proletariat. On 'Bloody Sunday', in January 1905, imperial forces fired on demonstrators in St Petersburg, killing hundreds. This led to protests throughout the empire, which escalated into revolution. Nicholas was forced to establish the State Duma, an elected legislature, as well as agree to Russia's first-ever constitution. He held on to power, and in the years after the 1905 Revolution solidified his rule by executing or imprisoning thousands of radicals. Twelve years later, another revolution swept through Russia, one which would overthrow imperial rule.

NOTABLE EUROPEANS: KARL MARX (1818–83)

Perhaps the most influential figure to emerge in the nineteenth century was Karl Marx; born into a middle-class Jewish family in the German city of Trier (at the time part of Prussia), he studied law and philosophy before beginning his career as a writer and journalist. In 1843 Marx moved to Paris, where he began to associate with communist and socialist groups. He also met his lifelong friend and collaborator

Friedrich Engels (1820–95), a German whose father was a wealthy textile manufacturer. Together they wrote *The Communist Manifesto*, published in February 1848. It argued that history was a process of class struggle. Capitalism had been created by the bourgeoisie overthrowing feudalism, while the future socialist society would be created by a revolution led by the proletariat. In 1849, following periods in Brussels and Cologne, Marx relocated to London, where he lived for the rest of his life. He and his family led a precarious existence, and were financially supported by Engels (who had also emigrated to Britain). In addition to journalism and activism, Marx had been researching and writing his masterwork *Das Kapital*, the first volume of which appeared in 1867 (the final two volumes were published posthumously, completed by Engels using Marx's notes). In his final decade, Marx suffered from health problems, limiting his ability to write. When he died in 1883, he was well known in leftist groups, but his influence was only truly felt in later decades. As the twentieth century dawned, Marxism would become the guiding philosophy for socialist movements across Europe and the world.

WINNING THE VOTE FOR WOMEN

The democratic movements of the Spring of Nations largely focused on winning the vote for men. It was not until the later nineteenth century that women across Europe began to agitate for their own enfranchisement. They were fighting against a patriarchal system that also limited their legal rights, access to education and role in the workforce. Associations and societies were formed across Europe, aimed at winning the vote for women. Opposing them were anti-suffrage movements that argued that women were too emotional and impulsive to vote. The first country in Europe to grant women the vote was Finland, which was part of the Russian Empire but had a high degree of autonomy. When the Parliament of Finland was established in 1906, women were given the right to vote and run for office. The next year, when the Finnish general elections were held, nineteen women were elected. The rest of the Nordic world followed in giving women voting rights: Norway in 1913, Iceland and Denmark in 1915, and Sweden in 1919. The First World War would be a watershed for the women's suffrage movement. As a result of the conflict, many women entered the workforce and played a significant role on the home front. This contributed to voting equality legislation being passed in several European states in the aftermath of the conflict, including Austria, Germany, Poland, the USSR, the Netherlands, Belgium and Luxembourg. The path to the ballot box was longer in many other European countries; women could not vote in Spain until 1933, in France until 1944, and in some parts of Switzerland until 1991.

The Second Industrial Revolution

The Second Industrial Revolution, which lasted from around 1870 to 1914, was characterized by advances in manufacturing, transport, communications and energy. Although Britain had at first been the leading industrial power, other European nations began to catch up, particularly Germany and France.

Before the nineteenth century, long-distance travel was slow and expensive. During the First Industrial Revolution, many European states had created networks of canals, which made carrying bulky goods easier. Roads were improved, but by modern standards they were rough and poorly maintained. The greatest improvements to land transport came from railways. The technology itself was not new – railways are simply tracks that wheeled vehicles run on. The earliest were powered by horses, humans or gravity. When steam-powered locomotives were run on tracks they could pull heavy loads remarkably quickly. They were developed in Britain during the early nineteenth century, and the first passenger railway, between Liverpool and Manchester, opened in 1830. The first railway in continental Europe opened in Belgium in 1835 and by the 1840s others had followed in France, Spain, Germany and the Netherlands. By 1900 a continent-wide railway network tied Europe together, economically and culturally. Steam was also used to power ships. From the 1840s, propeller-driven steamships were developed that could travel at more consistent speeds, making transoceanic travel more reliable and affordable (the invention of the steam turbine in 1884 made ships even faster).

Just as revolutionary as steam power was the internal combustion engine. Much of the early innovation in this field was in Germany, where in 1885 an internal combustion engine small enough to be fitted to a vehicle (first of all a bicycle) was developed. The next year Karl Benz (1844–1929) patented an engine to power an automobile, creating the first car. Due to its initially high cost, it would not be until the mid-twentieth century that the motor car took off as a vehicle for mass transport.

The introduction of electricity in Europe began in the 1880s and 1890s. It was used for lighting and to power factories and public transport systems. Electrical signals were also used to send messages along telegraph wires. During the second half of the nineteenth century, tens of thousands of miles of cable wire were laid across Europe. Messages could be sent near-instantly; in absolute terms the telegraph led to the greatest reduction of communication times in human history. The telegraph was swiftly followed by the telephone, which began to take off in Europe from the 1870s. Another innovation in communication was achieved in the 1890s by the Italian inventor Guglielmo Marconi (1874–1937), who used radio signals to communicate wirelessly.

Electrification, more efficient engines and cheaper steel were combined in factories that used moving assembly lines and interchangeable parts. Mass-production techniques rapidly increased productivity, decreasing the price of goods. This also led to workers being laid off because they were no longer needed or because their tasks could be done by less skilled employees. For those who remained, jobs were often more monotonous, with long hours imposed. By the later nineteenth century, a truly globalized economy had been created, with trade and banking tying the global economy together.

EUROPEAN IMPERIALISM

'New Imperialism' began in the mid-nineteenth century (as opposed to the 'Old Imperialism' of the fifteenth to eighteenth centuries that focused on the Americas), and saw European states establish colonies outside the continent,

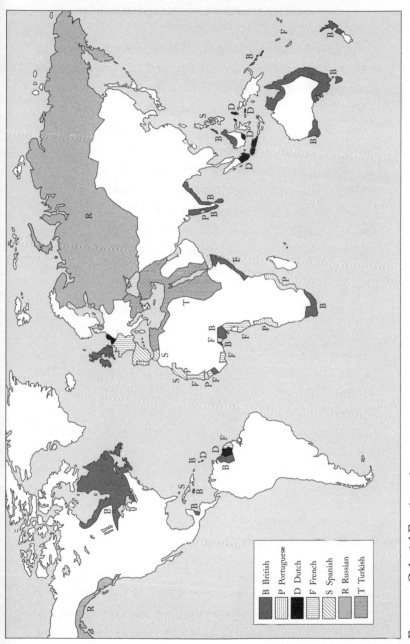

European Colonial Empires, 1822

B British		
P Portuguese		
D Dutch		
F French		
S Spanish		
R Russian		
T Turkish		

especially in Africa, Asia and Oceania. The two greatest rivals were Britain and France but other nations were involved, particularly Belgium, Italy, Germany, Spain and Portugal.

Much of the motivation for imperialism was economic. States aimed to secure markets for their industry as well as gain access to raw materials they could not produce or grow, like rubber, ivory and coffee. Many Europeans sought to 'civilize' other cultures by introducing their religious beliefs, technologies and social mores at the expense of indigenous customs. 'Scientific' racism was used to justify this, spuriously arguing that white Europeans stood at the apex of civilization, giving them the right to impose their rule and culture. Technological advances made imperialism possible. The steamship allowed faster oceanic travel, while the electrical telegraph allowed near-instant communication with the home country. The development of new medical treatments, particularly anti-malarial drugs, allowed Westerners to live in tropical climates. Weaponry such as the machine gun and high-powered artillery allowed European powers to bring overwhelming firepower to bear against indigenous peoples, even when outnumbered.

During the later nineteenth century, the greatest theatre for imperialism was Africa. From 1884 to 1885 thirteen European states (and the USA) met in Berlin to discuss the colonization of Africa. It was unilaterally decided that any European state could establish a colony in an unclaimed area of Africa as long as it notified others. This sped up, legitimized and formalized the 'Scramble for Africa' – by 1902, around 90 per cent of the continent was under European control. The Congo Free State symbolized the brutality of imperialism. Leopold II of Belgium (1835–1909) set up the Congo Free State in 1885 as a private territory under his control. Its only purpose was to extract resources, especially rubber, ivory and minerals. Leopold's private army forced people to work, using amputation on those who did not meet targets. Villages who did not comply were massacred. Congo's population dropped from twenty million to ten million. When these abuses were made public in 1908 the Belgian government began to rule Congo directly, ending some of the worst excesses of Leopold's regime.

CHAPTER 5

EUROPE IN CRISIS

THE TINDERBOX OF EUROPE

By the early twentieth century, Serbia, Montenegro, Greece and Bulgaria had all achieved independence from the Ottoman Empire. In spring 1912 they formed the Balkan League, an alliance under the patronage of Russia, which wanted to extend its influence in the region. Russia also encouraged Pan-Slavism, a movement that aimed to unify and win self-rule for Slavic peoples.

When the Balkan League was formed, the Ottomans were in the midst of fighting a war with Italy in the eastern Mediterranean. The conflict ended in October 1912 with the Ottomans ceding control of Libya and the Dodecanese islands. That month, the Balkan League declared war on the Ottomans, aiming to remove them from their last foothold in south-eastern Europe, which included Albania, Macedonia and Thrace. The First Balkan War was a disaster for the Ottomans. The Greek Navy dominated the Aegean Sea, preventing Ottoman reinforcements from arriving. Bulgarian forces advanced across Thrace, endangering Istanbul, while the Serbians and Montenegrins pushed into Albania and

Macedonia. The war ended in May 1913 with the Treaty of London, in which the Ottomans lost almost all of their European territory.

The Balkan allies disputed the division of their conquests. In June 1913, the Second Balkan War broke out when Bulgaria, seeking to win control of Macedonia, attacked Serbian and Greek forces there. The Bulgarians were driven back, with Montenegro joining the war against them. To make matters worse for Bulgaria, both the Ottomans and Romania invaded, seizing territory from them. Bulgaria opened peace negotiations. Under the resulting Treaty of Bucharest, the greater part of Macedonia was divided between Serbia and Greece (which also gained Crete), while Albania was made an independent principality. As the events of summer 1914 would show, the Balkan Wars did not end tensions in the region.

THE JULY CRISIS

On 28 June 1914, Archduke Franz Ferdinand (1863–1914), heir to the Austro-Hungarian throne, was assassinated during a visit to Sarajevo. Five weeks later, Europe was at war. How did the situation escalate so rapidly?

By 1914 Europe was divided into two power blocs. One was the Triple Alliance, composed of Germany, Austria-Hungary and Italy. Opposing them was the Triple Entente of Russia, France and the United Kingdom (Japan also joined them, but its involvement in the war was largely confined to Asia). Since the 1870s European powers had been building up their military capabilities; stockpiling arms and investing in new military technologies such as the machine gun, aeroplane and poison gas. Most states adopted conscription (the United Kingdom was an exception) and so had thousands of trained men in reserve. They could be called up and moved to strategic points under detailed mobilization plans. It was believed these plans would only be effective if they were initiated before the enemy's, so all sides craved to mobilize first to preserve the advantage. Exacerbating this was the 'Cult of the Offensive', the belief that the attacking force would have an overwhelming advantage. This shortened the window for diplomacy, as generals were convinced that landing the first strike was crucial. The most elaborate scheme was Germany's Schlieffen Plan, in which it would attack France though Belgium and Luxembourg. France's frontier defences would thus be bypassed and they would be quickly defeated, allowing Germany to then shift its energies east to Russia, which was expected to take months to fully mobilize.

Franz Ferdinand's visit to Bosnia-Herzegovina was highly controversial. Austria-Hungary had annexed the territory in 1908, much to the chagrin of those who wanted the South Slav lands to unify into a single state. There were numerous Pan-Slav groups, most of which received support from Serbia; they included Young Bosnia. One of their members, Gavrilo Princip (1894–1918), shot Franz Ferdinand and his wife, Sophie, Duchess of Hohenberg (1868–1914), while their car was driving through Sarajevo. Austria-Hungary held the Serbians partly responsible for the assassination, and was willing to go to war with them to prevent their promotion of Pan-Slavism. This risked angering Russia, a major supporter of Serbia's. Fortunately for the Austro-Hungarians, the German government assured them of its complete and total support, giving them a 'blank cheque' for acting against Serbia. Accordingly, on 23 July, Austria-Hungary issued an ultimatum to Serbia, ordering it to arrest people involved in the plot and end its support for Pan-Slav rebels. Though Serbia met almost all of the demands, Austria-Hungary still declared war on 28 July. This began a steady sequence of mobilizations and declarations. On 31 July, Russia initiated a general mobilization. The next day, Germany declared war on Russia and began to mobilize (as did France). Haste became crucial for Germany; it had to put the Schlieffen Plan into action for it to work. On 2 August, German troops entered Luxembourg and the next day invaded Belgium and declared war on France. The British government declared war on Germany on 4 August, as it had promised to defend Belgian neutrality under the terms of the 1839 Treaty of London. This also brought Commonwealth nations into the conflict.

At first there was great enthusiasm for the war. Jubilant crowds gathered across Europe's capitals, reserve forces met up with their units, and thousands joined the armed forces. It was confidently believed the war would be 'over by Christmas' – optimism soon to be dashed.

THE WESTERN FRONT, 1914–17

During Germany's invasion and later occupation of Belgium there were numerous atrocities against the civilian population, with thousands killed.

Eventually, German forces invaded northern France, closing to within fifty miles of Paris. At the First Battle of the Marne in early September, Franco-British forces counter-attacked and saved the capital; even using a fleet of Parisian taxis to deliver men to the front line. The opposing forces then attempted to outflank each other but their manoeuvres ended in stalemate. By the end of 1914, both sides had dug in to form defensive lines. The Western Front became a system of trenches (separated by No Man's Land) that stretched from the Swiss border to the North Sea. Due to machine guns, barbed wire and heavy artillery, defenders had a huge advantage, and going on the offensive attracted high casualties. Germany realized it could not deliver a knockout blow against France, so decided to fortify and follow a strategy of attrition.

While 1915 was generally a year of stalemate on the Western Front, 1916 saw violence on an unprecedented scale. Germany decided it would 'bleed France white' by inflicting huge casualties. It targeted the French stronghold of Verdun. In a brutal ten-month battle (the longest of the war) the French refused to withdraw, and pushed back the Germans. Over 300,000 died at Verdun. In the summer, the Allies launched a massed offensive in the Somme region, where the British made the principal effort. Although it did not reach all of its objectives, the Somme campaign relieved pressure on Verdun and placed a huge strain on German resources.

Germany went on the defensive in 1917. That March it withdrew to the Hindenburg Line, an elaborate system of fortifications with lines of barbed wire fifty miles deep, machine-gun nests and reinforced concrete emplacements. When France launched an attack on the positions, it was a costly failure and led to mass mutinies. The main fighting in the second half of the year was the Battle of Passchendaele; amidst the boggy morass of the damp, blasted Flanders landscape, the Allies made some gains but suffered huge casualties and were unable to make a decisive breakthrough. As 1918 dawned, an end to the fighting on the Western Front appeared distant.

TURKEY AND THE GALLIPOLI CAMPAIGN

On 2 August 1914, Germany and the Ottoman Empire signed an alliance. Germany would strengthen and help train the Ottoman military in return for being allowed movement through its territory. When the First World War broke out, the Ottoman Empire declared itself neutral, but within four months it was drawn into the conflict because of its alliance with Germany.

Turkey was the focus of an Allied invasion in early 1915. With stalemate in the West, the Allies launched an attack on the Gallipoli peninsula. They hoped it would be the prelude for an advance on Istanbul, and allow them to supply Russia from the south. The Gallipoli Front would be one of the greatest failures of the war. When British Empire and French ground forces landed in April, they established two beachheads, but suffered heavy casualties. They were unable to advance much beyond them, due to the rocky terrain, disease and fierce Ottoman defence. Allied troops began to withdraw in December, and the evacuation was completed by January 1916.

Ottoman forces carried on fighting in the Balkans, Caucasus and the Middle East. During the war there was a genocidal campaign of killings and deportations against Armenians in the empire, with Assyrians and Greeks likewise the focus of state violence. The Ottomans signed an armistice with the Allies in October 1918. In 1920 the Treaty of Sèvres was imposed on them. This dismantled the Ottoman Empire, with non-Turkish territories given independence. As a reaction to the harsh terms, an army officer called Mustafa Kemal (1881–1938) led a Turkish nationalist armed uprising that rejected Sèvres. It resulted in the overthrow of the final sultan, Mehmed VI (1861–1926), and the declaration of the Republic of Turkey in 1923. Its borders were recognized by the Allies under the Treaty of Lausanne. Kemal became president and passed a series of modernizing reforms; he was given the surname Atatürk, meaning 'Father of the Turks'.

The Italian Front and Rise of Mussolini

Italy had been part of the Triple Alliance but when the First World War broke out it declared itself neutral. The Italian government did not go to war because it saw the alliance as a defensive one that did not oblige it to take action if its partners had gone on the offensive. Furthermore, Italy had long-standing grievances with Austria-Hungary over its control of territories with significant ethnic Italian populations. In April 1915, Italy signed the secret London Pact with the Allies. The Italians agreed to switch their allegiance in return for Austrian territory and a protectorate over Albania that would be granted after victory was achieved. The next month Italy declared war on Austria-Hungary and invaded its territory. Fighting on the Italian Front was generally characterized by the same trench warfare as in the West but played out on rocky, mountainous terrain. Despite also facing German reinforcements in 1917, Italy emerged victorious from this 'mountain war', forcing Austria-Hungary to sign an armistice on 3 November 1918.

Although Italy ended the war on the winning side, many in the country regarded it as a 'mutilated victory', because Italy had not been given all of the territory it had been promised, and it was excluded from the carve-up of former German colonies. Italy had lost up to 650,000 dead and incurred heavy debts for little gain. The Italian Fascist movement, led by the former journalist and army veteran Benito Mussolini (1883–1945), capitalized on this sentiment and grew in popularity. Mussolini seized power in 1922 after the March on Rome, a massed demonstration of his supporters. He was initially prime minister but in 1925 adopted the title *Il Duce* ('The Leader'), turning Italy into a single-party dictatorship. Mussolini sought to make Italy the heir to the Roman Empire by building influence in the Mediterranean as well as gaining African colonies. From 1935 to 1936, Italy invaded and occupied Ethiopia, deposing its emperor and using aeroplanes, tanks and poison gas. For the moment, at least, it appeared Mussolini had triumphed.

RUSSIA AND THE EASTERN FRONT

The war started disastrously for the Russians. At the end of August 1914, they suffered a crushing defeat at the hands of the Germans at the Battle of Tannenberg (in modern-day north-eastern Poland). Russia was more successful in Galicia (a region now divided between Ukraine and Poland), where they made gains against Austro-Hungarian forces. During 1915 the Russian Army, which had too few munitions and an inadequate officer corps, was pushed back. Eventually,

Russia stabilized its position and ramped up its military industry, easing supply issues. In June 1916, Russia launched an offensive in Galicia. Although it attracted high casualties, strategically it was a great success and Austria-Hungary was only saved from disaster by German military intervention. With Austria-Hungary weakened, Romania joined the Allies, hoping to seize Transylvania. Entering the war was ultimately disastrous for Romania; despite Russian assistance, it was defeated and forced to surrender in December 1917.

The war grew unpopular among the Russian people, dissatisfied with the mounting death toll and food shortages. Nicholas II had made himself commander-in-chief, meaning he was tied to any military setbacks. As Nicholas was often away at the front line, he was insulated from his regime's unpopularity. His wife, Alexandra Feodorovna (1872–1918), served as regent, but due to her German birth she was the subject of public scorn and hatred. She had become a follower of a Siberian mystic, Grigori Rasputin (1869–1916), who had gained influence with the imperial family by claiming to be able to heal Nicholas and Alexandra's haemophiliac son. Rasputin's influence extended to matters of state, further undermining the tsarist regime. In December 1916, a group of dissatisfied nobles murdered Rasputin (it took a combination of poison, stabbing and shooting to finish him off), but his removal would not bring stability to Russia.

Discontent was widespread in Petrograd, which had been renamed when the war started as St Petersburg was perceived to be too German. The February Revolution (actually 8–16 March under the Gregorian Calendar in use in most of the rest of Europe – Russia still used the old Julian style and so was nearly two weeks behind) saw protests escalate into mass demonstrations. Order broke down as soldiers and police mutinied. Workers' councils called 'soviets' were set up across Russia – the largest and most important was established in Petrograd. With his authority in tatters, Nicholas abdicated. A provisional government was formed by the State Duma, although the Petrograd Soviet remained powerful. Russia remained committed to the war, and in July 1917 launched an offensive even though the authority of officers was undermined by 'soldiers' committees'. The attack was a failure; order in the Russian military broke down even further and the provisional government grew more unpopular. Another revolution dawned.

Vladimir Lenin (1870–1924) was a Russian communist leader who had been forced into exile in 1907, eventually settling in Switzerland. After the February Revolution, German authorities allowed him to travel home through their territories in a sealed train, hoping he would spread disorder in Russia. Lenin, who led a revolutionary socialist party called the Bolsheviks, decided another revolution was necessary, as he believed the provisional government was dominated by the bourgeoisie. In the October Revolution (which took place on 7–8 November), Lenin led an armed insurrection in Petrograd, which seized power for the Bolsheviks. He declared the Russian Soviet Federative Socialist Republic and announced they would end the war; a ceasefire was declared in the next month.

Peace talks with the Central Powers quickly broke down. In early 1918, Germany and Austria-Hungary advanced into Russian territory and forced them to accept harsh peace terms. Under the Treaty of Brest-Litovsk, signed on 3 March, Russia gave up Finland, the Baltic states, Belarus and Ukraine. The Soviet regime, which had moved the capital back to Moscow, was faced with a civil war against the White Army, a coalition of opposition groups supported by Allied powers, who sent money, supplies and reinforcements. Nicholas and the imperial family were executed in July as it was feared they would become figureheads of a counter-revolutionary movement. In 1919 the Red Army invaded Ukraine, where it fought the White Army and Polish forces. By the next year, the main component of the White Army had been defeated and peace was made with Poland in 1921. Fighting continued in eastern Russia until 1922, with the Red Army vanquishing the remaining opposition forces. That year the Union of Soviet Socialist Republics was declared, led by Lenin and initially comprised of Russia, Ukraine, Byelorussia, Armenia, Azerbaijan and Georgia (during the 1920s and 1930s it would be extended into Central Asia).

THE END OF THE WAR

From 1914 German U-boats had attacked shipping in the Atlantic, aiming to starve the United Kingdom into submission. Even neutral ships were targeted, which contributed to the USA entering the war on the Allied side in April 1917 (along with the revelation that Germany had made diplomatic overtures to Mexico about a potential alliance). American industrial strength and reinforcements provided a vital boost for the Allies.

With Russia defeated, in spring 1918 Germany embarked on a great offensive in the west, hoping to overwhelm the Allies before American manpower could be fully deployed. The Germans made initial gains, but were unable to hold them. Starting in August, the Allies led a massed counter-attack and, thanks to their numerical superiority and German exhaustion, they won a series of battles. During this 'Hundred Days Offensive', thousands of German soldiers surrendered as they steadily lost ground.

By the end of October, the military situation was hopeless for Germany. Its allies Bulgaria and the Ottoman Empire had already surrendered, while Austria-Hungary was on the verge of capitulating. Germany began to make initial peace negotiations. Despite the imminent end of the war, the German Admiralty ordered a final attack on the Royal Navy in the North Sea. Sailors stationed in northern Germany, unwilling to take part in such a futile and purely symbolic effort, mutinied. Over the next week, revolt spread across the war-weary country. On 9 November, socialist members of the Reichstag declared Germany a republic. Kaiser Wilhelm II (1859–1941), with the Germany Army in Belgium, abdicated and went into exile in the Netherlands.

The new German government signed an armistice with the Allies at 5 a.m. on 11 November. The ceasefire began six hours later and German forces withdrew east of the Rhine. As the Allies had never actually invaded Germany, a myth arose that they had not been truly defeated, but 'stabbed in the back' by domestic revolutionaries. The final terms of the peace were still to be decided, but the First World War was finally over – it had killed over 8.5 million military personnel.

The Treaty of Versailles

The Paris Peace Conference opened on 18 January 1919. Although twenty-seven countries were formally involved, the 'Big Four' of France, the United Kingdom, Italy and the USA largely dominated. While the American president Woodrow Wilson (1856–1924) idealistically strove for a moderate settlement with Germany, the French and the British sought to impose more punitive measures. The Treaty of Versailles was signed on 28 June. Germany, which had no say in the terms, submitted to huge reparations, lost its colonial empire, gave up territory in Europe, and had to limit its armed forces in the future. The Rhineland region was to be demilitarized and occupied by the Allies for fifteen years. Under the 'War Guilt' clause, Germany had to accept full responsibility for starting the war.

The fate of Austria–Hungary, which was also made to take responsibility for the war's outbreak, was also considered. Under the Treaty of Saint-Germain-en-Laye, signed on 10 September, it was to be broken up. The treaty created the new Republic of Austria and the independent states of Hungary, Czechoslovakia and Poland. In the Balkans, where the spark for the conflict had been lit, there were also major changes. Shortly after the war had ended, Serbia had joined with Montenegro. As a result of Saint-Germain-en-Laye this state linked up with former Austro-Hungarian territories in the Balkans to form the Kingdom of Serbs, Croats and Slovenes (renamed Yugoslavia in 1929). This fulfilled the dreams of those who had wanted an independent South Slav state. Under the Treaty of Neuilly-sur-Seine, signed in November

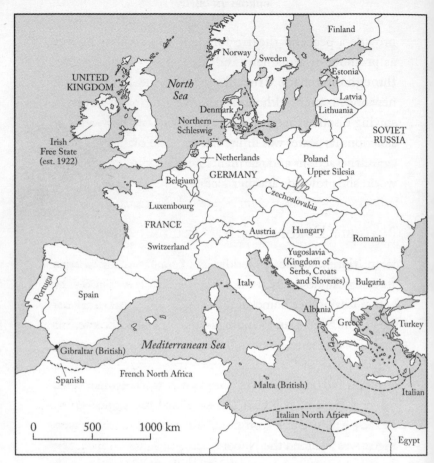

Europe After the First World War

1919, Bulgaria (which had joined the Central Powers in 1915) lost territory to Greece, Yugoslavia and Romania and had to pay reparations. Finally, the Treaty of Trianon, signed in June 1920, dealt with Hungary; fixing its borders to leave it landlocked, and limiting its armed forces.

As a result of the talks in Paris, the League of Nations was founded on 10 January 1920. It was designed to provide a peaceful theatre for collective security as well as promote disarmament and the settlement of disputes through diplomacy. Crucially, the USA never joined this new organization. Although it enjoyed some early success in solving disputes, because the League was unable to impose sanctions its power was limited. It stood helpless against the aggressive actions and rearmament of the 1930s that saw the world slide towards another global conflict.

Notable Europeans: Marie Curie (1867–1934)

Born Maria Salomea Skłodowska in Warsaw, Curie began studying clandestinely at the underground 'Flying University' before leaving her homeland in 1891 for Paris to further her education. She began attending lectures at the Sorbonne, and started working as a research scientist. In 1894 she met the French physicist Pierre Curie (1859–1906); they married the next year and began working together; in 1898 they discovered two new elements, polonium (named after Poland) and radium. In 1903 Marie Curie won her doctorate and together with Pierre was awarded the Nobel Prize for Physics in 1903. She was the first woman to win a Nobel. Tragedy struck in 1906 when Pierre slipped while crossing the road and was run over by a horse-drawn cart, causing a fatal fracture of his skull. Marie Curie continued her work, becoming a professor at the Sorbonne and winning another Nobel Prize, for Chemistry, in 1911. During the First World War she worked to develop mobile X-rays that could be used to treat soldiers near the battlefield. Marie Curie's years of working with radioactive materials led to her death in 1934.

WEIMAR GERMANY AND THE RISE OF HITLER

As Germany recovered from the First World War, it faced a wave of leftist uprisings. The largest was in Berlin, led by the communist Spartacus League (named after the leader of the ancient Roman slave rebellion). The provisional government turned to the army and the *Freikorps*, nationalist militias, to restore order. Elections for a national assembly were held in January 1919 (German women voted for the first time). As Berlin was still in upheaval, the assembly met in Weimar, nearly 50 miles away, where it drew up a constitution that established Germany as a democratic parliamentary republic.

German government finances were in a parlous state because the country had borrowed heavily to finance the war. This was worsened by war reparations, which had to be paid in gold or foreign currency. When Germany fell behind, Franco-Belgian forces occupied the industrial Ruhr Valley in 1923 so they could levy goods instead of cash. Hyperinflation made the German currency worthless; by November it took over four trillion marks to buy one US dollar. Germany was delivered from financial chaos by reforms that re-stabilized the currency and modified the reparations.

A fascist group founded in Bavaria, the National Socialist German Workers' Party (better known as the Nazis), saw this as a chance to seize power. Its leader, the Austrian-born Adolf Hitler (1889–1945), an army veteran who had fought on the Western Front, attempted to stage a coup by leading a march from Munich to Berlin. The 'Beer Hall Putsch' of November 1923 failed miserably; Hitler was arrested and found guilty of high treason but only imprisoned for one year. For the rest of the 1920s Germany was politically and economically stable. This period of calm was brought to an end by the Wall Street Crash of October 1929, which led to the Great Depression of the 1930s. It was the most widespread and serious economic crisis of the century, causing a breakdown in international trade and mass unemployment.

The crisis was a gift to the Nazis. Their membership swelled as Hitler toured the nation making speeches and holding rallies. His promises to tear up the hated Treaty of Versailles, combined with his anti-semitic and nationalist rhetoric, appealed to a population eager for a scapegoat. The 'Brown Shirts', Nazi paramilitaries, violently suppressed political rivals. In July 1932, the Nazis became the largest party in the Reichstag, and Hitler became chancellor in January 1933. The next month the Reichstag was burned down by a lone Dutch communist. Hitler exploited the fire to impose repressive decrees that consolidated Nazi power. After elections in March the Nazis were again the largest party, although they did not hold a majority. Thanks to support from the conservative German National People's Party, they pushed through an Enabling Act that allowed them to change the constitution. Hitler transformed Germany into a single-party fascist state, and made himself *Führer* ('Leader') with sweeping powers. Trade unions were abolished and racist and anti-semitic laws were passed to ensure the ethnic 'purity' of the nation. A secret police force called the Gestapo kept order, while political enemies were purged in the 'Night of the Long Knives' in 1934. As the rest of Europe would find, Hitler's plans for Germany had even more wide-ranging effects.

IRISH INDEPENDENCE

The Irish Home Rule movement grew in size and influence during the later nineteenth century. Many Protestants, concentrated in the north of the country, grew to reject home rule, as they believed it would lead to Catholic dominance. Conversely, Irish republicanism, which demanded complete independence, became more influential. After several failed attempts, in 1914 the parliament in Westminster passed legislation that would have given Ireland home rule. However, when the First World War broke out the act was suspended. In Easter 1916, Irish republicans staged a rising in Dublin. The British put down the rebellion in six days, executing many of its ringleaders. In 1919 guerrilla war broke out between Irish republicans and the United Kingdom. Peace was made in 1921; the treaty created the Irish Free State as a self-governing dominion within the Commonwealth. The six counties with significant Protestant populations were given the option to remain part of the United Kingdom, which they duly did – becoming Northern Ireland. The treaty split the Irish republicans, many of whom rejected partition. In June 1922, the Irish Civil War broke out between pro- and anti-treaty forces. By May 1923, the pro-treaty side had emerged victorious. In 1949 Ireland became a republic, officially severing links with the Commonwealth and British Crown.

Notable Europeans: Albert Einstein (1879–1955)

Born into a middle-class Jewish family, Einstein grew up in southern Germany, becoming fascinated with mathematics and physics during his teens. In 1896 he enrolled at the Swiss Federal Polytechnic in Zürich, having renounced his German citizenship to avoid military service (he was stateless until being granted Swiss citizenship in 1901). After graduating in 1900, Einstein was unable to win an academic position and so went to work at the Swiss patent office in Bern. He continued to ponder scientific questions. In 1905, his 'miracle year', Einstein published four papers that would revolutionize physics, transforming the perception of the universe, and he was also awarded his doctorate by the University of Zürich. He rose to prominence, finally winning academic positions, going on international lecture tours, and from 1913 to 1933 serving as director of the Kaiser Wilhelm Institute for Physics at the University of Berlin. He developed the theory of relativity, which explained how particles interacted and the laws of gravitation, and won the Nobel Prize in Physics in 1921. The rise of the Nazis made Einstein the focus of anti-semitic attacks.

In 1933, when Hitler became chancellor, Einstein was visiting the USA. With his career and life in peril, he decided not to return to Germany and took up a position at the Institute for Advanced Study in Princeton, New Jersey, becoming an American citizen in 1940. During the Second World War Einstein's work (particularly his famed equation $E=mc^2$) helped lay the theoretical foundations for the splitting of the atom. In 1939 Einstein, who was a pacifist, signed a letter to President Roosevelt recommending that the USA should develop an atomic bomb. After it was deployed in 1945, Einstein was part of the global campaign to stress the dangers of atomic warfare. During his last decade, he worked on developing a 'unified field theory' that would unify all the laws of physics. He was never able to finish it, dying as a result of heart complications in 1955.

THE RISE OF STALIN

Under Lenin's leadership, the USSR became a single-party state. Potential enemies were purged in the Red Terror, while land was forcibly redistributed and major industries nationalized. In 1921 Lenin introduced the 'New Economic Policy', which allowed some free enterprise with the aim of stimulating an economy stricken by years of war. A growing force was the Georgian Joseph Stalin (1878–1953), who in his younger years had raised money for the Bolshevik cause by bank robbery. Stalin had played a major role during the civil war and was elevated to General Secretary of the Communist Party of the USSR in 1922. Lenin often disagreed with Stalin and was concerned about his growing power but illness prevented him from acting against him. In 1924 Lenin died after a series of strokes; in his honour Petrograd was renamed Leningrad.

Lenin was succeeded by a troika made up of Stalin and two other Soviet politicians, Lev Kamenev (1883–1936) and Grigory Zinoviev (1883–1936). Stalin's main opponent was Leon Trotsky (1879–1940), leader of the Red Army during the civil war. Trotsky led a faction that believed the socialist revolution should be spread worldwide. Stalin favoured the policy of 'Socialism in One Country' – that the USSR should focus on strengthening itself. Kamenev and Zinoviev sided with Trotsky but Stalin marginalized them, making himself sole leader. Trotsky was forced into exile, settling in Mexico where he was assassinated by a Soviet secret police agent in 1940.

Stalin abandoned the New Economic Policy in 1928 and implemented the First Five-Year Plan, designed to rapidly industrialize the USSR. Collective farms were established and (often unrealistic) targets were imposed on factories. As a result of this policy (and drought), agricultural production declined, leading to famine from 1932 to 1933, which killed over six million. Around two-thirds of the deaths were in Ukraine; as it had resisted Stalin's policies, his government deliberately worsened conditions there, leading to mass starvation. Stalin then instituted the Second Five-Year Plan, which ran from 1933 to 1938. It focused on heavy industry and improving transport infrastructure. Although his position was secure, in 1936 Stalin began a purge of any perceived opponents. During this 'Great Terror', show trials were held where suspects were forced to make false confessions; both Zinoviev and Kamenev were found guilty at such courts and shot. Hundreds of thousands were executed or sent to gulags – isolated prison camps where they were forced to work in harsh conditions. By 1938 the wave of violence had subsided; Stalin's dominance was absolute.

The Spanish Civil War

Spain had remained neutral during the First World War, and in 1931 it became a republic after the constitutional monarch was deposed. In February 1936, the Popular Front, a coalition of left-wing parties, won the Spanish elections. That July a group of right-wing nationalist army officers attempted to overthrow the government. The coup failed to win total control of the country, instead leaving it divided between zones controlled by the Republicans, who supported the democratically elected government, and the military-backed Nationalists. Spain quickly descended into civil war.

General Francisco Franco (1892–1975) emerged as the leader of the Nationalists. He wanted to establish an authoritarian, socially conservative regime, with himself as dictator. The Spanish Civil War became symbolic of the struggle between fascism and democracy, and both sides looked overseas for assistance. While the Republicans had thousands of foreign volunteers join their cause, they found little formal support from other states, except for Soviet Russia. In comparison, the Nationalists were actively backed by Italy, Germany and Portugal. They provided formal military support and training, volunteers, and supplied weapons and vehicles.

The Nationalists made steady gains as the Republicans succumbed to infighting. By 1939 the war was coming to an end. The Republican stronghold of Barcelona fell in January and Madrid followed in March. On 1 April 1939, Franco declared victory; thousands of his enemies were executed or imprisoned, or fled into exile.

The Outbreak of the Second World War

Hitler's foreign policy violently disrupted Europe. He was determined to annex all territory where ethnic Germans lived as well as to gain *Lebensraum* ('living space') for his people by conquering territory in the east. He tore down the restrictions of Versailles; stopping reparation payments, building up German military strength, and reoccupying the Rhineland in 1936. Europe's great powers adopted a policy of appeasement in the face of Hitler's policies. They stood idly by during the *Anschluss* ('joining'), when Austria was annexed by Germany in March 1938 – something forbidden by Versailles. Hitler's next ambition was to take the Sudetenland, a region of Czechoslovakia with a majority ethnic-German population. Under the Munich Agreement that September, Italy, France and the United Kingdom permitted Germany to annex the Sudetenland. This was not the limit of German ambitions on Czech territory; in March 1939 they occupied the rest of the country and carved it up among themselves, Hungary, Poland and the newly created Nazi client state of Slovakia.

Hitler then turned his focus on Poland. With his actions growing more and more provocative, the United Kingdom and France allied with Poland, pledging to protect its independence if Germany invaded. On 23 August the USSR and Germany shocked the world by announcing a non-aggression pact, which included secret clauses about how Central and Eastern Europe was to be divided between them (the treaty paved the way for the Red Army's occupation of the previously independent Baltic republics of Estonia, Latvia and Lithuania in June 1940, which were annexed into the USSR the next month). This Molotov–Ribbentrop Pact was a prelude to Germany's invasion of Poland, launched on 1 September, and beginning the Second World War. Two days later, France and the United Kingdom (and the Commonwealth nations) declared war on Germany. They were unable to save Poland. German forces cut through their lines and in mid-September the Red Army invaded from the east. Fighting in Poland ended on 6 October; it was then divided between Germany, the USSR and Slovakia.

For the next six months there was an uneasy equilibrium, leading some to dub the conflict the 'Phoney War'. Relative calm was brought to an end on 9 April 1940, when Germany invaded Denmark and Norway. Denmark fell after a one-day campaign, while Norway held out until June. Both countries fell under German occupation until 1945. On 10 May the Germans unleashed their Blitzkrieg tactics against France and the Low Countries (as well as the British Expeditionary Force that had been sent across the Channel). In one week the Netherlands was occupied and by the end of the month Belgium had surrendered. France was caught by surprise as the Germans invaded though the hilly, forested Ardennes region, long considered impassable to tanks. This bypassed the Maginot Line, France's system of fortified border defences. The German advance split the Allies; over 300,000 were stranded in northern France and only saved by a heroic evacuation from Dunkirk. On 10 June Germany's ally Italy declared war against the Allies and invaded southern France. The French government fell, and a new regime led by Philippe Pétain (1856–1951), a general during the First World War, signed an armistice on 22 June. Germany occupied northern

France (including Paris) and coastal areas on the Channel and Atlantic; Italy occupied some territory in the south-east; and Pétain ruled the unoccupied zone as a German puppet state from the town of Vichy. The United Kingdom, now led by a coalition government headed by Winston Churchill (1874–1965), faced invasion. However, Germany was unable to gain the aerial and maritime dominance over the Channel necessary to ferry troops to England. Even so, Germany appeared to be on the verge of total dominance over Europe.

THE EASTERN FRONT

There remained one great foe for Hitler to face: the USSR, the great bastion of communism, the implacable ideological enemy of Nazism. Flouting their non-aggression pact, Germany and the other Axis powers prepared for invasion. Their plans had to be delayed for over a month due to the Balkan Campaign, which saw the Axis win control of Albania, Greece and Yugoslavia. Despite occupying these areas, the Axis faced sustained opposition from local resistance groups.

On 22 June 1941, an Axis force of over 3.6 million invaded the USSR along an 1,800-mile front. It was mainly German, although it included troops from their allies in Romania, Finland, Italy, Hungary, Slovakia and Croatia (Spanish and Portuguese volunteers also took part). Their aim was to conquer the European part of Russia by the end of October, before winter truly set in. The advance moved in three main groups: through the Baltic states towards Leningrad, through Belarus towards Moscow, and through Ukraine to the oil fields of the Caucasus. Despite repeated warnings,

Stalin had refused to believe an attack would happen, so Soviet defences were wholly inadequate. Their resistance was swamped by an Axis advance of over fifty miles a day. The Red Army's weapons were inferior and it was poorly led because thousands of experienced officers had been liquidated during Stalin's Great Purge. The Eastern Front would be the most brutal and ferocious theatre of the Second World War. Nearly half of its deaths took place there, and massacres of civilians were frequent. Both sides used scorched-earth tactics, leaving the countryside in ruins.

After the early shock of the invasion, the USSR rallied. The Axis were unable to capture Leningrad, which survived more than two years' siege. Attacks on Moscow were repulsed, and Soviet war industries were relocated east, out of the range of enemy bombers. By winter 1941–2, the Axis advance had slowed. Behind their lines they faced armed opposition; their harsh treatment of the population in captured Soviet territory encouraged partisan activity that was a constant scourge. In summer 1942, the Axis launched an offensive aimed at capturing the oil fields of Azerbaijan. Standing in their way was Stalingrad (now Volgograd) in south-western Russia, a city that was a major centre of industry and a transport hub. The battle for the city symbolized the carnage of the Eastern Front. The Axis attack began in August 1942, reducing the city to rubble. There followed a bitter street-fight among the ruins where the Red Army narrowly held on until the Soviet counteroffensive that winter.

Axis forces in Stalingrad were encircled, and forced to surrender in February 1943. The Axis never regained the initiative on the Eastern Front, and manpower dwindled as their supply lines were dangerously stretched. In summer 1943, the Axis launched a major offensive against the Soviets at Kursk in the largest tank battle in history. German forces attacked ferociously and made some gains but the Soviets held out and regained territory. Kursk was the final major Axis offensive in the east. After the battle the Red Army advanced steadily west. By the end of 1944, they had retaken the Baltic states, and were poised to enter Poland and East Prussia.

THE TURNING OF THE TIDE

On 7 December 1941, Japan attacked the American naval base at Pearl Harbor in Hawaii. The following day the USA declared war on Japan, joining the Allied effort in the Pacific. On 11 December, Germany and Italy, who had concluded a military alliance with Japan the previous September, declared war on the USA. This would have far-reaching implications for Europe. The USA, which had already been supplying the Allies with weapons, vehicles and supplies, was able now to fully deploy its manpower, economic strength and vast industrial resources against the Axis.

American reinforcements helped the Allies win control of North Africa by May 1943. This allowed them to turn their attention to Italy. Sicily was invaded on 9 July and captured after a six-week campaign. The Allies then landed on the Italian mainland and pushed north. The Italian king, joined by senior government and military officials, deposed and imprisoned Mussolini and signed an armistice with the Allies on 3 September. In response German forces moved into Italy. Mussolini was rescued from captivity and installed as the ruler of a Nazi puppet state in the north, the Italian Social Republic. Fighting in Italy continued until May 1945, although the month before the war ended Mussolini was captured by communist partisans, who summarily executed him and had his corpse strung up in public in Milan.

On 6 June 1944, the Western Allies invaded France. On D-Day, 156,000 Allied troops landed in Normandy (by sea and air) in one of the most ambitious military operations of all time. They established a beachhead and pushed into the interior of France. Charles de Gaulle (1890–1970), a general who had led the forces of Free France from exile became chairman of the provisional government. In Germany a conspiracy arose to assassinate Hitler and launch a coup, but on 20 July he survived the explosion of a bomb planted at his headquarters in East Prussia. After the attempt, the Nazi regime arrested and executed thousands of potential opponents.

By October most of France and Belgium had been liberated. Hitler's last throw of the dice was to attack a vulnerable position in the Allied lines in the Ardennes. In the ensuing Battle of the Bulge, the Germans expended most of their remaining resources but were ultimately repulsed. By February 1945, the Allies were on the offensive once more, and poised to advance into Germany.

The Holocaust

Hitler played on centuries of prejudice against Jewish people by blaming them for many of Germany's problems. According to him, they were both responsible for the spread of communism and part of a shadowy international conspiracy to control the world economy. Spurious pseudoscience was used to claim that the Jews were *Untermenschen* ('subhumans'); racially distinct from the superior Aryan race. Several other groups were believed to be 'undesirable' and would later be the focus of Nazi persecution, including the Roma, Slavs, the mentally and physically disabled (who were often subjected to forcible sterilization) and homosexuals.

The anti-semitic ideology of the Nazis became the law of the land. On 15 September 1935, the Reichstag enacted the Nuremberg Laws. The 500,000 German Jews were stripped of their citizenship. They were also forbidden to marry or have sexual relations with people who were not Jewish. Later legislation forbade Jews from voting and holding public office. Their passports were stamped with a red 'J' and they were forced to take Jewish names (Israel for men, Sarah for women) to make them easier to identify. On *Kristallnacht* ('Night of the Broken Glass'), a state-sponsored pogrom that took place in November 1938, Jewish businesses, properties and places of worship were attacked and vandalized. In this hostile atmosphere, many Jews attempted to flee the country, but most European governments were unwilling to accept refugees. Many wished to settle in Palestine, where since the later nineteenth century the Zionist movement had tried to establish a Jewish homeland. The British authorities that ruled the Holy Land limited Jewish migration, believing it would destabilize the region.

During the Second World War, millions of Jews fell under Nazi rule. In Eastern and Central Europe, Jews were packed into over a thousand ghettos, while in the west they were forcibly registered. On 20 January 1942, senior Nazi leaders met at Wannsee in the Berlin suburbs. They decided to begin the 'Final Solution' to the 'Jewish Question' – their total elimination. At first the Nazis had used *Einsatzgruppen* ('task forces'), paramilitary death squads, to hunt down and kill Jews (and other undesirable groups) in conquered territory. The victims were gunned down, but after Wannsee the Nazis transitioned to genocide on an industrial scale. Concentration camps were set up across Eastern Europe, to which Jews in Nazi-controlled areas would be deported. There they would be forced to work. Those who the Nazis did not need for labour were killed in gas chambers and cremated.

There was resistance to the Holocaust. Underground organizations and courageous individuals attempted to smuggle Jewish people to safety. Many went to partisan groups, where they fought against the Nazis. In April 1943, the Warsaw Ghetto rose up against the Nazis, barricading streets and holding out for over a month before their resistance was wiped out. There were numerous other uprisings and challenges to Nazi extermination, but they were usually brutally put down. As the war was coming to an end and the Nazis went on the retreat, they dissolved the ghettos and camps, killing the inhabitants or forcing them to march west, with many dying or murdered along the way.

As the Allies advanced into Nazi territory, the true horror and scale of the camps was uncovered. The German leadership would be held accountable. At Yalta it had been decided war criminals would be put on trial. As a result, the Nuremberg Trials were held to publicly reveal Nazi crimes and prosecute the political, economic and military leadership responsible.

The Nuremberg trials began in November 1945 and were heard before an international tribunal with Soviet, British, American and French judges. Similar trials continued until 1949. They revealed the true scale, horror and brutality of the genocide that had killed over six million Jewish people.

THE END OF THE SECOND WORLD WAR

On 16 January 1945, Hitler moved into the *Führerbunker*, an underground complex in Berlin. His mental and physical health deteriorated as his enemies advanced into Germany from both sides. In February the 'Big Three' Allied leaders (Churchill, Stalin and Roosevelt – de Gaulle was not invited) met at Yalta on the Black Sea to discuss their plans for post-war Europe. At the conference it was agreed that Germany would be placed under Allied occupation; and it would be subjected to the 'Five Ds' (denazification, demilitarization, deindustrialization, democratization and decentralization). Furthermore, democratic regimes would be established in all liberated nations, and free and fair elections held. Two months after Yalta, Roosevelt died of a cerebral haemorrhage; Vice President Harry S. Truman (1884–1972) led the USA through the rest of the war.

In mid-April, the Red Army broke into the Berlin suburbs. On 30 April Hitler, realizing defeat was inevitable, committed suicide. Berlin fell to the Soviets two days later. A new Nazi government was formed in Flensburg in northern Germany. Its authority dwindled away in the face of the Allied advance. Early on 7 May, the German High Command signed an unconditional surrender – all of their forces would cease military operations the next day. Victory in Europe Day was publicly announced late on 8 May (although in the USSR and much of the east of the continent it was already the next day). Nearly six years of violence had left most of Europe in ruins and led to the deaths of over forty million soldiers and civilians.

There was still much to be settled. There were Soviet forces across Eastern and Central Europe, and Stalin had already established a friendly communist government in Poland. Hence, there was already considerable tension between the Soviet Union and the Western Allies when they gathered outside Berlin for the Potsdam Conference, which began on 17 July (as with Yalta, de Gaulle was not invited). The occasionally fractious talks continued until 2 August. It was agreed that Allied forces would occupy Germany, with the United Kingdom, USA, France and the USSR all establishing their own areas of control. Berlin was likewise divided into four zones (the same would apply to Austria and Vienna). It lay within Soviet-controlled East Germany. Reparations would be seized from occupied areas, and lands Germany had annexed would be returned. Poland was a particularly contentious subject. It was given former German territory in East Prussia but, in a stunning betrayal of the Polish government-in-exile and earlier promises of democracy, Stalin's puppet regime was recognized as legitimate. Similarly, the USSR would create satellite states in much of the rest of Eastern and Central Europe, with single-party communist rule instituted in Albania, Bulgaria, Czechoslovakia, Hungary, Romania and, later, East Germany. In Yugoslavia a federal people's republic was proclaimed in November, led by the communist partisan leader Josip Broz Tito (1892–1980).

While the fighting in Europe was over, the war in Asia was still ongoing. As part of the Potsdam Agreement, the USSR declared war on Japan on 2 August, and invaded Manchuria. Japan finally surrendered on 2 September, following American nuclear strikes on Hiroshima and Nagasaki.

With the Second World War finally over, steps were taken to avoid such a conflict in the future. The United Nations (UN) was officially established on 24 October, as an organization to promote and keep peace and foster international cooperation. Unlike the ineffective League of Nations, which was disbanded, the UN was a powerful and influential organization, and far more successful in its founding aims. Despite this, over the next four decades Europe would be split by another conflict, the Cold War.

CHAPTER 6

CONTEMPORARY
EUROPE

The Beginning of the Cold War

As the Second World War came to an end, a different (and far longer) conflict began. It became known as the Cold War and pitched the capitalist-democratic West, led by the USA, against the communist East, led by the USSR. The two superpowers were both armed with nuclear weapons that, had they been deployed, would have brought worldwide destruction. In their rivalry both the Soviets and Americans formed global alliances that eventually created two power blocs. Instead of fighting each other, both sides often fought proxy wars where they gave support to allies, hoping to place friendly regimes in power. This geopolitical and ideological struggle divided Europe between East and West, with an 'iron curtain' separating the two sides.

The first armed conflict of the Cold War occurred in Greece. As the Axis occupation ended, different groups in the Greek Resistance vied to fill the power vacuum. In late 1944, the uneasy alliance between communist and royalist factions broke down, leading to violence in Athens. Churchill was determined to keep communists out of power, and deployed

British forces against them, leading to their disarmament in February 1945. In the aftermath, there was widespread violence and killings of left-wingers. Elections were held in March 1946, while that September a referendum approved the retention of the monarchy. The communists boycotted both polls, claiming they were rigged. A guerrilla war broke out between communists and government forces. The USSR avoided directly supporting the communists, but they did receive backing from Albania, Bulgaria and Yugoslavia. In contrast the British actively backed the government until rising costs forced them to withdraw their aid in 1947, with the USA stepping in to replace them. It took until 1949 for Greek government forces to win victory. The war had damaged Greece even more seriously than the Axis invasion and occupation, and the fighting led to the displacement of over 500,000 people.

The American desire to block Soviet dominance of Europe meant that they committed to maintaining a long-term military presence there. In March 1947, President Truman announced that it would be American policy to support 'free peoples' resisting totalitarian regimes. This 'Truman Doctrine' became a driving force of American foreign policy, and saw them provide arms, military backing and funds for anti-communist groups around the world. In addition to backing for government forces in the Greek Civil War, the USA also sent financial aid to Turkey to ensure that Soviet shipping would not be allowed to pass through the Turkish Straits from the Black Sea to the Mediterranean.

The American government began the four-year European Recovery Program, better known as the Marshall Plan, in

1948. It provided 13 billion dollars of financial assistance to seventeen European nations, with the United Kingdom, France and West Germany (see below for details on the partition of the country) receiving the most. The USSR was offered the chance to participate but declined, and also refused to let its satellite states in Eastern Europe receive any money either. The plan was hugely successful in helping to rebuild the shattered European economy, contributing to growth and increasing trade between nations.

No area of Europe was more contentious than Germany, which remained under Allied occupation. In the west, the USA, United Kingdom and France planned to merge their occupation zones to form a single federal republic. As part of the Marshall Plan, West Germany was financially stabilized, and in June 1948 given a new currency, the Deutsche Mark. This was anathema to the USSR, which aimed to keep the German economy weak. Stalin reacted to the currency reforms by announcing a blockade of West Berlin, preventing all road and rail traffic into the part of the city occupied by the Western Allies. West Berlin was cut off from the world, with just one month's supply of food left. Stalin announced the blockade would end when the new Deutsche Mark was withdrawn. The Western Allies refused to back down, and launched a massive airlift to West Berlin. Aircrews worked around the clock, while local citizens helped to unload supplies. Stalin, unwilling to spark a war, did not order that the aircraft be shot down. The blockade continued into the winter but the flights carried on, delivering at their peak six thousand tons of supplies a day, preventing West Berlin from collapsing. The USSR lifted the blockade in May 1949.

NATO

A further sign of the growing division in Europe was the formation of the North Atlantic Treaty Organization (NATO), which was formed in April 1949. With Soviet military forces stationed across Eastern and Central Europe, Western powers decided they needed to create a formal alliance to oppose them. NATO was a system of collective security, where member states agreed to come to the defence of each other if they were attacked. The founder signatories of the agreement were Belgium, Denmark, France, Iceland, Italy, Luxembourg, Netherlands, Norway, Portugal and the United Kingdom; joined by Canada and the USA. In 1952 Greece and Turkey were admitted, with West Germany joining in 1955. The formation of NATO meant that there were two heavily armed forces on European soil, primed for the outbreak of a mass land war that, thankfully, never arrived.

THE BEGINNING OF EUROPEAN INTEGRATION

After the Second World War, many European nations turned towards international cooperation, and built bridges between states that often had long histories of war and rivalry. On 9 May 1950, France's foreign minister, Robert Schuman (1886–1963), made a speech mooting the possibility of pooling French and West German coal and steel production. This declaration led to the 1951 Treaty of Paris, which established the European Coal and Steel Community (ECSC) between not just France and West Germany but also Belgium, the Netherlands, Luxembourg and Italy. By signing the agreement, the leaders of the six countries agreed to create a common market for coal and steel between them. Not only would this reduce competition for these vital natural resources, it would make war between them highly unlikely because it would tie their economies closely together. A 'Common Assembly' was set up where representatives from the ECSC could meet; at this stage it was a consultative body and a forum for discussion with no legislative power. Also established as part of the Treaty of Paris was the European Court of Justice. The ECSC would be the first of a succession of supranational institutions that would grow in influence and importance, and also bring in an increasing number of European states.

After the establishment of the ECSC its member states moved forward with further integration. In 1957 they signed the Treaty of Rome, establishing the European Economic Community (EEC), which aimed to work towards the creation of a single market between the six states, where trade barriers would be removed for all products and a shared set of tariffs on imported goods imposed. In addition, the European Atomic Energy Community (Euratom) was created to establish a common market for nuclear power and its safe and peaceful development. The Common Assembly of the ECSC became the European Parliamentary Assembly, meeting for the first time in 1958 in Luxembourg, and was later renamed the European Parliament. Also established that year was the European Commission, which acted as the EEC's executive and was comprised of commissioners from each member state. The first major new initiative of the EEC was the Common Agricultural Policy, which aimed to stabilize food supply, set prices and support farming. The EEC was not uncontroversial, as many politicians believed it would infringe on their national sovereignty. De Gaulle, the President of France, was particularly vocal in his opposition. In 1965 he withdrew French representatives from the EEC's councils until a compromise was reached whereby members could use a veto against policies that impinged on their national interest. Integration moved forward: the Brussels Treaty, which came into effect in 1967, merged the governing bodies of the ECSC, Euratom and the EEC; together they were known as the 'European Communities'. The next year all tariffs between members of the EEC were removed.

There were moves towards enlargement. In 1961 Denmark, Ireland, Norway and the United Kingdom all applied to join the European Communities. De Gaulle vetoed the applications in 1963 as he believed British membership would be a vehicle for the USA to extend its influence over Europe. After de Gaulle resigned as president in 1969, his veto on allowing Danish, Irish, Norwegian and British membership was lifted. Accordingly, the countries (with the exception of Norway, which opted out of joining after a referendum) all joined the European Communities in 1973. The great European venture was gathering pace.

The German Miracle

In 1945 Germany lay in ruins, its economy shattered. As a result of Cold War rivalries, the country was formally divided in 1949, when the Allied occupation ended (although tens of thousands of troops remained stationed there). The eastern part became a Soviet satellite state, the German Democratic Republic, while in the west the Federal Republic of Germany was created. The divergent paths of East and West Germany starkly illustrated the malign impact of communist rule. Although East Germany had a strong economy compared to the rest of the Eastern Bloc, it was quickly outpaced by West Germany. The first post-war Chancellor of West Germany was Konrad Adenauer (1876–1967), the former mayor of Cologne who had been arrested and imprisoned by the Nazis in 1944 after the failed assassination attempt against Hitler. After his election as leader of West Germany in 1949, Adenauer built ties with former enemies and paid reparations to Israel for the Holocaust. Under his leadership, the West German economy was transformed. In addition to the new currency, the Deutsch Mark, price controls were removed and tax rates cut. The West German government, which was based in the city of Bonn, used funds from the Marshall Plan to make loans to companies to help them reconstruct. As a result of these policies, and buoyed by millions of workers fleeing west from East Germany, the West German economy rebounded, rapidly becoming one of the strongest and most dynamic in Europe. So dramatic was West Germany's growth that it became known as the *Wirtschaftswunder* ('economic miracle').

CHANGE IN THE USSR

After the Second World War, Stalin was determined to achieve security for the USSR through dominance of Eastern Europe. The exception was in Yugoslavia – although it was a communist state, its leader Tito often clashed with Stalin. In 1948 Tito and Stalin's disagreements led to Yugoslavia's expulsion from Cominform, the body set up by the USSR to coordinate Europe's communist parties. Tito continued to forge his own path and in 1961, along with India, established the Non-Aligned Movement – a group of nations that sought to be independent from any power bloc.

Stalin expanded the USSR's military capabilities, increasing the size of its armed forces and overseeing the development of nuclear weapons in 1949. The cult of personality around him, which portrayed him as an all-knowing national father, was encouraged. As he aged, Stalin became more paranoid. In September 1952, he had several Kremlin doctors arrested, tortured and killed on the groundless suspicion they planned to assassinate Soviet leaders. Most of those accused were Jewish, and it is likely Stalin planned on using this 'Doctors' Plot' as part of a larger campaign of anti-semitic policies and purges. Before he could enact his plans, he was struck down by a cerebral haemorrhage on the night of 1–2 March 1953. He died four days later.

Stalin did not leave concrete succession plans. Senior figures decided to institute a system of collective leadership. Initially, the dominant figure was Georgy Malenkov (1902–88), who led both the government and the party. However, the ruling Council of Ministers quickly decided too much power had been concentrated on Malenkov. He continued as head of government but was replaced as party leader by Nikita Khrushchev (1894–1971). A power struggle began, which saw Khrushchev emerge as the sole national leader by the end of 1953. He reversed many Stalinist policies, denouncing their brutality, freeing millions of political prisoners and moving towards democratization. In 1955 he agreed to end the occupation of Austria, which became a neutral democratic republic.

Khrushchev survived a 1957 internal attempt to overthrow him. Later that year the USSR fired an intercontinental ballistic missile and launched the first space satellite. This created an arms and space race with the USA, which along with the 1962 Cuban Missile Crisis dangerously strained relations between the two superpowers. Global calamity was averted through negotiation, and in 1963 the USSR, USA and the United Kingdom signed the Partial Nuclear Test-Ban Treaty, which banned above-ground testing of nuclear weapons. Despite this, in 1964 there was another plot to remove Khrushchev. He was unable to maintain the confidence of the Soviet leadership and was forced into retirement.

Leonid Brezhnev (1906–82) was Khrushchev's successor. In 1975 he was a party to the Helsinki Accords, a declaration signed by thirty-three European states (plus the USA and Canada) that fixed the boundaries of Europe. Brezhnev's decision to invade Afghanistan in 1979 had major repercussions. The war, combined with heavy military spending, placed a huge strain on the USSR that contributed to its eventual break-up.

THE EASTERN BLOC IN THE 1950S AND 1960S

On 14 May 1955, the USSR and its seven satellite states signed the Treaty of Friendship, Cooperation, and Mutual Assistance in Warsaw. This solidified Soviet control over the region, allowing it to garrison troops in its satellites, and acted as a counter to the growing force of NATO. There had been challenges to Soviet hegemony. In June 1953, prior to the signing of the Warsaw Pact, construction workers in East Berlin went on strike. This escalated into a national wave of protests and industrial action, which was violently countered by the East German police and Red Army.

The Warsaw Pact did not prevent political upheaval in the Eastern Bloc. In October 1961, protests in Poland led to the installation of a new reformist leader, Władysław Gomułka (1905–82). The Soviet government allowed him to stay in power, and increased Polish autonomy. Gomułka led Poland for fourteen years. He became more authoritarian, culminating in 1968, when he repressed student protests and approved of anti-semitic campaigning that led to the emigration of thousands of Polish Jews. Events in Poland encouraged anti-Soviet dissenters in Hungary. Students in Budapest marched through the streets, igniting a revolution that overthrew the government. The new prime minister, Imre Nagy (1896–1958), announced he would restore free elections and withdraw Hungary from the Warsaw Pact. The USSR sent in the Red Army to crush the new regime. Nagy was arrested (and eventually executed) and the more compliant János Kádár (1912–89) was installed as leader; he ruled until 1988 and instituted a system of gradual reform with elements of free-market economics known as 'goulash communism'.

Berlin was the focus of a clash between the USSR and the West in 1961. Although the border between the two Germanys was closed, thousands had fled communist rule by entering West Berlin. The USSR wished to close off this exit, and in June Khrushchev demanded Western forces withdraw from West Berlin. On 13 August, East German authorities began laying barbed wire and concrete blocks around West Berlin. When finished the Berlin Wall was nearly a hundred miles in length, and heavily guarded to prevent any attempts to scale it, the wall remained a symbol of Europe's ideological divide.

In January 1968, Alexander Dubček (1921–92) became national leader of Czechoslovakia. He announced a new direction called 'socialism with a human face'. The economy would be liberalized, freedom of speech granted, and steps taken to democratize the political system. The 'Prague Spring' ended in August, when the USSR (along with Bulgaria, Hungary and Poland) invaded and occupied. The action was justified under the 'Brezhnev Doctrine', which stated the USSR could militarily intervene in communist nations they believed were deviating from the correct path. Dubček was forced to roll back his reforms and resigned the next year. Even within the Eastern Bloc the invasion was controversial. The Romanian leader Nicolae Ceaușescu (1918–89) criticized the USSR's actions. Albania went even further: its leader Enver Hoxha (1908–85) withdrew his country from the Warsaw Pact in protest. The events of 1968 showed that the USSR was still more than willing to use force to continue its dominance of its satellites.

EUROPEAN DECOLONIZATION

Just a handful of European colonies still remain. They are mostly small island territories in the Caribbean and South Pacific, the last vestiges of various colonial empires that once spanned the world. Decolonization gathered pace after 1945 as European powers, often near-bankrupt as a result of the Second World War, gave their colonies independence. In some places, wars of national liberation were fought to win self-rule when European colonial governments refused to relinquish control. Furthermore, there was often violence and political instability in newly independent states.

The United Kingdom had built the largest empire. From 1931 to 1947 it had given independence to Canada, Australia and New Zealand. South Africa had also gained sovereignty in 1934, although its black majority was disenfranchised. British rule of the Indian subcontinent ended in 1947, following decades of protest. It was divided along religious lines, leading to the creation of the separate states of India and Pakistan. Partition displaced millions and led to mass violence that killed hundreds of thousands. In 1948 Burma (now Myanmar) and Ceylon (now Sri Lanka) won independence and British forces withdrew from Palestine. That year a communist insurgency against British rule in the Federation of Malaya began. Fighting continued after the federation won independence as Malaysia in 1957, not ending until 1960. British rule in Africa ended during the 1950s and 1960s; the process was often violent – as in Kenya where thousands of Mau Mau rebels were killed. Although Egypt had been independent since 1922, the United Kingdom (and France) invaded the country in 1956 to prevent the nationalization of the Suez Canal. International pressure forced them to withdraw after a week, signalling the end of the United Kingdom's status as a superpower. Jamaica won independence in 1962, and over the next three decades it was followed by the other British possessions in the Caribbean. British colonies in the Pacific became independent during the 1970s. Finally, in 1997 Hong Kong was returned to China.

France attempted to retain its overseas colonies. This led to conflict with pro-independence groups in Indochina, which had been occupied by Japan during the Second World War. France was forced to give independence to Cambodia and Laos in 1953 and, following a crushing defeat at Điện Biên Phủ in 1954, withdrew from Vietnam (which was split between north and south, laying the seeds for the subsequent American intervention and civil war there that lasted until 1975). In Africa, France attempted to vanquish independence movements, often using force – particularly in Madagascar, Algeria and Cameroon – but by 1962 had been compelled to give up control of most of its colonies on the continent.

Smaller European imperial powers also decolonized. Following a nationalist revolution, the Dutch East Indies became independent as Indonesia in 1949. Suriname, in South America, followed suit in 1975, but the Dutch Caribbean islands still remain part of the Kingdom of the Netherlands. Belgian imperial rule ended in Congo in 1960 and in Burundi and Rwanda in 1962. Equatorial Guinea, a Central African territory ruled by Spain, won independence in 1968. One of the longest independence struggles was the Portuguese Colonial War, which lasted from 1961 to 1974, and led to Portugal's African colonies winning their independence. Elsewhere, Portugal gave up control of East Timor in 1975 and Macau in 1999.

CHANGE IN PORTUGAL AND SPAIN

In 1926 the Portuguese First Republic was overthrown in a military coup. Six years later, António de Oliveira Salazar (1889–1970), previously a successful finance minister, became prime minister. He oversaw the creation of the conservative, nationalist and authoritarian *Estado Novo* ('New State') regime, established in 1933. It used censorship, imprisoned political opponents and banned opposition parties. He maintained Portuguese neutrality during the Second World War, and remained president until suffering a cerebral haemorrhage in 1968. By then Portugal was in the midst of an unpopular and costly military struggle to retain its African colonies. These wars led to a group of anti-war military officers launching a coup that overthrew the *Estado Novo* in 1974. This 'Carnation Revolution' (so-called due to its peaceful nature) led to a new regime that ended the colonial wars and held free elections, paving the way to political stability and eventual entry into the EEC.

Shortly after the *Estado Novo* ended, change came to Spain. After winning the Civil War, Franco had repressed opposition and censored the press. His attempts to make Spain self-sufficient stalled economic growth and left the country on the brink of famine. During the 1960s and

1970s, Spain opened up to foreign investment and rapidly industrialized. Franco held power until he died of heart failure in 1975. The monarchy was then restored under Juan Carlos I (b. 1938) and free elections were held in 1977. The democratically elected government survived an attempted coup in 1981, when rebel Civil Guards held parliament and ministers captive for eighteen hours. Juan Carlos publicly denounced the coup, which quickly fizzled out, solidifying Spain's successful transition to democracy.

FURTHER ENLARGEMENT OF THE EEC AND THE CREATION OF THE EU

In June 1979, the first elections for the European Parliament (whose members had previously been appointed by national parliaments) were held in the nine countries of the EEC, with seats allocated according to population – although smaller states are given more representation. These were the first international elections, and have been held every five years since then, although voter turnout has often been low – regularly dipping below half the electorate in many countries. Members of the European Parliament do not sit according to their country of origin, but are arranged into blocs according to their political party. Since its inception, the powers and responsibilities of the European Parliament have grown, and it now has responsibility for many legislative and budgetary matters.

The 1980s saw further expansion of the EEC into southern Europe, with Greece joining in 1981, and Portugal and Spain following in 1986. That year the Single European Act was signed, committing member states to establishing a single market between them by the end of 1992. This act gave the EEC greater powers to break down trade barriers and set policy over areas of common concern such as the environment and consumer rights.

The European Union was established in 1993. It was created by a treaty drafted by EEC members in the Dutch city of Maastricht in December 1991, which was signed two months later. Maastricht renamed the EEC the 'European Community', reflecting that its scope had extended beyond economic matters, and made it the 'first pillar' of the EU. The other two pillars were a shared foreign policy and cooperation in criminal matters. The two architects of this epochal move towards further integration were the German chancellor Helmut Kohl (1930–2017) and the French president François Mitterrand (1916–96), whose close partnership symbolized the reconciliation between their two nations that they hoped would help guarantee lasting peace in Western Europe. Not all European leaders were so enthusiastic about integration – for example, the British prime minister Margaret Thatcher (1925–2013) grew increasingly suspicious of the EU during the 1980s, fearing it would become a Brussels-led 'super-state'. Maastricht also set criteria for applicant countries: they were required to be free-market democracies willing to accept EU law. Accordingly, Austria, Finland and Sweden were all admitted into the EU in 1995 (Norway again rejected joining following a referendum). As the new millennium dawned, the EU was poised for further expansion and integration.

THE COLLAPSE OF THE USSR

By the 1980s, the USSR was choked by a sclerotic bureaucracy, overburdened by defence spending, and economically stagnant. Brezhnev's health was flagging. Already suffering from a wide range of ailments, he had a stroke in May 1982 and a fatal heart attack that November. His replacement was the KGB chief Yuri Andropov (1914–84); after suffering renal failure he died in February 1984. His successor was Konstantin Chernenko (1911–85), a conservative with lung and heart problems who died in March 1985. His successor was Mikhail Gorbachev (b. 1931), a younger man with plans for reform.

Gorbachev was willing to meet this challenge. His two main initiatives were *glasnost* and *perestroika*. Meaning 'openness', *glasnost* encouraged the Soviet government to listen to the concerns of citizens, and allowed limited freedom of the press. *Perestroika* ('restructuring') aimed to overhaul the USSR's political and economic system. In an attempt to reverse economic stagnation, elements of the free market were introduced, with private ownership and foreign investment permitted. However, the state retained a high degree of control and the economy continued to be sluggish. Gorbachev moved towards democratization, with multi-candidate elections for local positions (the Communists remained the only legal political party).

Liberalization fed the growth of nationalist sentiment in the fifteen republics that made up the USSR. Anti-regime protests were violently repressed, as in Georgia, when on 9 April 1989 the Red Army attacked demonstrators in Tbilisi, killing at least twenty people and injuring thousands more. In the Baltic republics, pro-independence groups were particularly strong and well organized. On 23 August 1989, protestors in all three states joined hands to form the Baltic Way, a human chain of two million people over four hundred miles long, as a symbol of their desire for self-rule.

Gorbachev's reforms gathered pace. In March 1990, he created a new position with executive powers for himself: President of the Soviet Union. That month he also amended the USSR's constitution to allow political parties other than the Communists to exist. Hundreds of new parties sprang up overnight. On 12 June 1990, the Congress of People's Deputies of the Russian Soviet Federative Socialist Republic declared their desire to establish a democratic constitutional state and stated their laws had precedence over the USSR's. The declaration was signed by Boris Yeltsin (1931–2007), chairman of the Russian Supreme Soviet, a former ally of Gorbachev's who had become one of his leading critics. That year, symbolizing the declining influence of communism, the people of Leningrad voted to change the name of their city back to St Petersburg.

Gorbachev struggled to impose his reforms and policies, facing opposition from both nationalist groups and conservatives in his party. In August 1991, as he was preparing to implement decentralizing reforms that would give more power to the republics, Communist Party hard-liners tried to seize power. Gorbachev was held captive at his summer residence in Crimea. The attempted coup petered out after Yeltsin, from the steps of Russia's parliament building, denounced the plotters and called for Gorbachev's restoration. Gorbachev duly returned but his authority had evaporated. By the end of the year all of the constituent republics of the USSR had declared independence. On 25 December, Gorbachev resigned as leader, and the USSR was dissolved the next day.

THE 1989 REVOLUTIONS

During the 1980s there was mounting dissatisfaction in the Eastern Bloc. Poland saw the first of the decade's challenges to communism, when in 1980 there were nationwide protests against high food prices. In Gdańsk seventeen thousand shipyard workers went on strike. On 31 August, their leader, Lech Wałęsa (b. 1943), an electrician, reached an agreement with the Polish government that gave unions the right to organize and strike as well as other conditions that improved the lives of workers. Solidarity was formed on 22 September, the first independent trade union in the Eastern Bloc. By early 1981 ten million people had joined. They appealed for further reforms, leading to the Polish government declaring martial law in December 1981. Solidarity was declared illegal, its leaders were arrested and it was dissolved in October 1982.

Nineteen-eighty-nine would be the year popular protests and civil resistance led to revolution and permanent regime change. Hungary's communist government was forced to begin talks with opposition groups in April, which led to major reforms. The Republic of Hungary was declared on 23 October and free multi-party elections held in May 1990. Meanwhile, the border fence with Austria was dismantled, allowing thousands of Hungarians (as well as East Germans and Czechoslovaks) to travel to the West during the spring and summer of 1989. In Poland, partially free parliamentary elections were held in June. The previously outlawed Solidarity movement won virtually all of the seats it was allowed to contest. Free presidential elections followed in 1990. Solidarity leader Wałęsa was elected president, and oversaw Poland's transition to democracy.

The East German government could not repress the increasingly common and widespread peaceful pro-reform demonstrations. On 9 November it was announced that it was legal to enter West Germany. That evening thousands of East Berliners flocked to the wall that divided their city. The overwhelmed border guards allowed them over the wall, which began to be hacked down by the gathering masses. The symbol of the Iron Curtain lay in ruins as jubilant Berliners celebrated. Free elections were held in East Germany on 18 March 1990, and Germany was reunified that October. Kohl, who had been Chancellor of West Germany since 1982, became the leader of the reunified nation, retaining the position until 1998. He oversaw the first stage of reunification, including the moving of the capital from Bonn to Berlin, although there remain significant economic disparities between the east and west of Germany.

During the last three months of 1989, communist rulers fell in Bulgaria, Czechoslovakia and Romania. In Bulgaria Todor Zhivkov (1911–98), who had led the country since 1954, was forced to resign on 10 November, and free elections were held in June 1990. In Czechoslovakia, after a student march in Prague on 17 November was violently suppressed by the police, protest swept the nation. Within six weeks the communist government gave up power. On 29 December, the playwright and dissident Václav Havel (1936–2011) became president, and elections were held the following June. This Velvet Revolution (so-called because of its smooth nature) was succeeded by the 'Velvet Divorce' of 1993; the peaceful separation of the Czech Republic and Slovakia.

The final great event of 1989 was in Romania. On 21 December, Ceaușescu addressed a rally in Bucharest. The crowd began heckling and booing him, showing the public's growing disdain for the man who had repressively ruled Romania since 1965. Rioting and violence broke out across the country. Ceaușescu and his wife (who was also deputy prime minister) were captured by the army and tried before a military tribunal. Both were found guilty of crimes against the nation and executed. As the new decade dawned, democracy was emerging across Eastern and Central Europe.

Post-Soviet Russia

On 8 December 1991, as the USSR was disintegrating, the leaders of Belarus, Russia and Ukraine signed the Belavezha Accords. This declared that the USSR would be replaced by the Commonwealth of Independent States (CIS). Barring the Baltic states, all the former republics of the USSR joined the CIS. On 21 December, the Alma-Ata Protocol was signed, which formally founded the CIS and declared Russia the official successor-state of the USSR. The CIS was a far looser confederation than the USSR, aiming at economic, political and security coordination.

There was warfare across the former components of the USSR. In 1988 fighting had broken out in Nagorno-Karabakh, which was part of Azerbaijan but had a majority Armenian population that wished to secede and unite with Armenia. This escalated into a six-year war that involved both the Azeri and Armenian governments. Nagorno-Karabakh became de facto independent but is internationally recognized as being part of Azerbaijan. Likewise, in South Ossetia and Abkhazia in Georgia there were separatist wars that ended in their de facto independence. Finally, in 1992, following four months of fighting, the Transnistria region of Moldova became a de facto independent state.

The nascent Russian Federation was in chaos. It faced massive budget deficits, precipitous drops in productivity, high rates of inflation, rampant organized crime and mass unemployment. Nationally owned industries were privatized, leading to the emergence of an oligarchy that had purchased huge state assets at cut prices. In April 1993, Yeltsin, facing widespread criticism, won a referendum that showed the majority of voters had confidence in his leadership. Yeltsin continued to clash with the Russian parliament, and in October used the army to put down resistance to his rule. That December, a new constitution that strengthened the power of the president was approved by referendum. Thanks to loans from the International Monetary Fund, oil and natural gas incomes, and currency reforms, Yeltsin stabilized the Russian economy. But his popularity steadily declined as for many people their financial position was still insecure, with standards of living inferior to those they had enjoyed under communism.

Many of Russia's regions demanded more autonomy, and often fought wars to secure it (as well as using terrorist attacks against civilians). The most serious fighting was in Chechnya, a majority-Muslim region in the North Caucasus. In 1994 Yeltsin sent troops into the region to prevent it breaking away – they were forced to withdraw after two years, meaning Chechnya won de facto independence. Following the Second Chechen War (1999–2009), Russia regained control over the area. There was also separatist violence in the nearby regions of Dagestan and Ingushetia, which both remained part of the Russian Federation.

In August 1999, Yeltsin selected Vladimir Putin (b. 1952), a former KGB officer who had entered Russian politics in 1996, as his prime minister. After Yeltsin resigned as president on 31 December, Putin replaced him. He then won the presidential elections of March 2000 and has dominated Russian politics since then. Putin's main aim has been to restore Russian power, as well as bring order and prosperity. Under his rule, the Russian economy has stabilized but he has used repressive tactics and violence against his opponents. Putin has sought to strengthen Russian influence abroad. In August 2008, Russia invaded Georgia, which had become increasingly close to the West, in support of Abkhazian and South Ossetian independence. After five days of fighting, Russia recognized the independence of both regions, and established military bases there. Russia intervened in Ukraine, opposing mass protest movements in the country that had sought to strengthen ties with the West. In February 2014, Russian forces began to make incursions into Ukraine. Despite international opposition, Crimea was annexed in

March, and Russia still provides support for separatist rebels in the Donbass region. Putin continues to enjoy widespread popularity among the Russian public, comfortably winning the March 2018 presidential elections.

THE YUGOSLAV WARS

On 4 May 1980, Tito died. During his long period in power, he had entrenched single-party rule and his own authority, while also creating a federal system that decentralized some powers to the six constituent republics of Yugoslavia (Bosnia and Herzegovina, Croatia, Macedonia, Montenegro, Serbia and Slovenia). Following Tito's death, Yugoslavia had a collective presidency whose chairmanship rotated among the leaders of the six republics. During the 1980s, the Yugoslav economy faltered, with high levels of inflation and unemployment. This gave succour to nationalist groups. On 25 June 1991, Croatia and Slovenia announced they were seceding from Yugoslavia. The Yugoslav army attempted to prevent Slovenian secession, but was defeated after a ten-day war that ended with Slovenia's independence. Macedonia voted for independence in a referendum, and it peacefully became an independent state on 8 September.

Elsewhere in the former Yugoslavia, the path to independence was more traumatic. Croatia's Serb minority broadly did not want to become part of an independent Croatian state and, supported by the Yugoslav army, launched an armed uprising. In March 1992, Bosnia and Herzegovina declared independence. The make-up of this republic was complex, as it was divided between Bosnian Muslims (known as Bosniaks), Catholic Croats and Orthodox Serbs. Bosnian Serbs wanted their own state, and began fighting to secure as much territory as possible. Similarly, Bosnian Croats also used force to try to forge their own state. On 27 April, Serbia and Montenegro formed a new federation between themselves that was dominated by the Serb president Slobodan Milošević (1941–2006). The Yugoslav Wars were the most savage and bitter conflict Europe had seen since the Second World War. Hundreds of thousands of people became refugees, ethnic cleansing was commonplace, and there were numerous massacres – most infamously in Srebrenica, where Bosnian Serbs killed eight thousand Bosniaks. By the end of 1995, the wars in Croatia and Bosnia and Herzegovina had ended (in the latter country the largely autonomous Republika Srpska was established in majority-Serb areas).

In 1998 conflict broke out in Kosovo, which was part of Serbia but had a majority ethnically Albanian Muslim population. Milošević attacked pro-independence rebels, killing civilians and displacing thousands. In response to the gathering humanitarian crisis, NATO intervened in March 1999, bombing Serbia and Montenegro for three months until Milošević agreed to withdraw. Subsequently, a UN-peacekeeping force was sent into Kosovo, which declared independence in 2008. Milošević was voted out of office in 2000, then arrested on suspicion of corruption and extradited to The Hague to stand trial for involvement in war crimes. He died in his cell of a heart attack before a verdict was reached. The final Yugoslav republic to secure independence was Montenegro, which, following a referendum, dissolved its federation with Serbia on 3 June 2006.

CERN

The European Organization for Nuclear Research (better known as CERN, an abbreviation derived from its French name, *Conseil européen pour la recherche nucléaire*) was established in 1954 in an attempt to stop the best scientific minds moving to the USA. Based in a vast research facility located outside Geneva, CERN is devoted primarily to the study of particle physics. According to its charter, CERN's work must not be concerned with military requirements. The organization has grown from twelve founding states, which all contribute to its costs and decision-making, to twenty-two members (all are European states with the exception of Israel, which joined in 2014). Countless breakthroughs that have transformed the understanding of the universe have been made at CERN. Perhaps the most important was the proof of the existence of the Higgs boson, which was theorized to give all particles mass. It was detected in 2012 at CERN by means of the Large Hadron Collider, an underground seventeen-mile ring of superconducting magnets that shoot particle beams at each other. Also developed at CERN was the World Wide Web (WWW). Its inventor was the English engineer Tim Berners-Lee (b. 1955), who first proposed the WWW in 1989 as a method for scientists around the world to share information. Four years later the software behind the WWW was released into the public domain; it would transform society.

The Euro and Eastern Expansion of the EU

The EU created a European Single Market, with free movement of capital, labour, goods and services. The Treaty of Maastricht also encouraged further integration through the creation of the Economic and Monetary Union (EMU) within the EU. This would bring the economies of member states together by setting common trade and financial policies. The central part of the EMU was a common EU currency, known as the euro. Countries would have to meet strict conditions to adopt the euro and take part in the EMU, including limiting inflation, public debt and government deficits. In 1998 the European Central Bank was founded; based in Frankfurt, it would administer the euro and set monetary policy. That year it established the conversion rates between the euro and the eleven EU countries (Austria, Belgium, Finland, France, Germany, Ireland, Italy, Luxembourg, Netherlands, Portugal and Spain) that had joined. The British and Swedish governments declined to participate, and the Danish public rejected membership in a 2000 referendum. Greece was allowed to join in 2001, after making wholesale changes to its economy and state finances. Following a three-year transition period, euro notes and coins entered circulation on New Year's Day 2002.

Following the fall of the Iron Curtain, many states in Central and Eastern Europe were eager to adopt EU membership. However, senior figures in the EU were reluctant to allow them to join immediately, fearing that adding a raft of less economically developed countries would be destabilizing. Eventually, in 2004, eight formerly communist countries were allowed to join the EU (Czech Republic, Estonia, Hungary, Latvia, Lithuania, Poland, Slovakia and Slovenia), along with the Mediterranean island states of Cyprus and Malta. Since then, Slovenia, Cyprus, Malta, Slovakia and the Baltic states have all adopted the euro. The EU expanded further in 2007, when Bulgaria and Romania joined, with Croatia following suit in 2013.

In December 2007, following talks in Lisbon, the Maastricht Treaty was amended. The Treaty of Lisbon extended the powers of the European Parliament and took steps to further unify EU foreign policy. It formalized the European Council, a body made up of the leaders of the member states that shaped the EU's priorities and political agenda. Under the treaty, the Charter of Fundamental Rights became legally binding across the EU, guaranteeing every one of its citizens a wide range of inalienable freedoms. Article 50 of the Lisbon Treaty would prove to be crucial, as it detailed the process of a country voluntarily leaving the EU. The prime mover in the Lisbon negotiations was Angela Merkel (b. 1954), who in 2005 became the first woman elected Chancellor of Germany (she has remained in power since then but plans to stand down in 2021), and has become the most powerful leader in the EU. However, before the Treaty of Lisbon could come into force, all EU members had to sign it. At first it was rejected in Ireland following a referendum in June 2008, but after gaining some concessions, the country agreed to it after holding another referendum in October 2009. The next month the Czech president signed the treaty after his country's courts determined it was compatible with their constitution. As it had been ratified by all member states, the Treaty of Lisbon came into force on 1 December.

EUROPE AND THE GLOBAL FINANCIAL CRISIS

In 2007 a collapse in the American sub-prime mortgage market (where millions had been granted risky loans to buy property) forced the Lehman Brothers investment bank to file for bankruptcy in 2008, and brought several other major financial institutions to the verge of collapse. Economic instability spread to Europe, where several banks failed and the stock market crashed. Iceland was particularly badly hit. The economy of the sparsely populated island in the North Atlantic had traditionally been focused largely on fishing, but after banking deregulation in 2001 it had developed a large financial sector. Three major Icelandic commercial banks had rapidly expanded and taken on billions in foreign debt, but when global trust in them failed, they collapsed. The Icelandic krónur swiftly depreciated, and the government was forced to turn to the International Monetary Fund for financial support to stabilize their economy.

The global recession created serious problems in Europe, leading to high unemployment (particularly among the young), banking crises, increased government debts and falling productivity. In the eurozone, the crisis was particularly serious, as instability in one member could damage all of those that used the currency. Also, the fact the European Central Bank had to set interest rates and fiscal policies for the entire eurozone curbed the ability of individual governments to make economic changes tailored

The Growth of the European Union

to their own needs. In 2010, to prevent financial collapse,
Cyprus, Greece, Ireland, Portugal and Spain were all forced
to take out loans funded by other eurozone countries, the
European Central Bank and the International Monetary

Fund. One of the conditions for receiving this money was to impose harsh austerity policies that entailed massive reductions in government spending (such cuts were also commonplace in many other European states). This was often highly unpopular, especially in Greece, where there were mass protests and riots against austerity. It led to the rise of Syriza, a populist coalition of radical and left-wing groups that initially opposed austerity but was forced to make severe cuts after coming to power in 2015. In Spain, protests against austerity led to the founding of a new left-wing populist party, Podemos (from Spanish for 'we can'), which within a year of its founding became the third-largest political party in the country in the 2015 general elections. Despite the gravity of the global financial crisis, European economies have resumed growth in its aftermath.

EUROPE IN CRISIS?

Since the global financial crisis, there has been growing dissatisfaction with the status quo in Europe. For some, Europe's greatest problem is migrants, particularly from war-torn Africa and the Middle East. In 2015 around one million people sought refuge in Europe. Many parties have run on anti-refugee policies, appealing to voters by claiming migrants are responsible for social ills and promising to limit their numbers or refuse to accept them.

Right-wing populism, often nationalist in tone, has risen in influence. Nationalist and anti-establishment parties have grown in popularity, for example in France and Italy. This trend has also been particularly powerful in the former

Eastern bloc, such as in Hungary and Poland. Euroscepticism is often central to populist political parties (both right-wing and left-wing). These groups are opposed to not just the EU but also European integration. Their main criticism of the EU is that it is an opaque and overly bureaucratic institution that erodes national sovereignty. This is often tied to anti-immigrant and nativist language. Euroscepticism has made its greatest impact on the United Kingdom, where a referendum on EU membership was held in 23 June 2016, where 52 per cent of those who voted opted to leave the EU. As a result, the British government triggered Article 50 of the Treaty of Lisbon on 29 March 2017, setting a two-year limit for negotiating the United Kingdom's withdrawal from the EU. The exit negotiations between the British government and EU leadership have been fractious and controversial, leaving many doubts about the future relationship between the United Kingdom and Europe.

Twenty-first-century Europe will face a number of fundamental problems, such as maintaining order and social cohesion while society becomes increasingly polarized in the face of globalization and the automation of many economic sectors, resolving the problem of low fertility rates that will lead the population to decline, finding a way to address climate change, and the risk of conflict in the former USSR. In spite of these, and other, potential difficulties, there is reason to be optimistic. Europe, particularly in its western part, remains one of the most wealthy, democratic, and developed regions of the world, as well as continuing to foster technological and artistic innovation. Furthermore, as this book has shown, Europe has been beset by periodic warfare between its major powers, and although there have been major outbreaks of violence, since the end of the Second World War the continent has generally experienced one of the most peaceful and prosperous periods in its history, which, if lessons from the past are heeded, should continue long into the future.

ACKNOWLEDGEMENTS

I'd like to thank Gabriella Nemeth and everyone at Michael O'Mara Books for all of their hard and expert work in the preparation of this book. Also, thank you to all my students and colleagues at Massey, Waikato, and Cambridge for the discussions and insights about European history.

INDEX

Page numbers in *italics* refer to maps